Published by Bracketpress
183 Dunkirk Rise College Bank Way Rochdale Lancashire OL12 6UJ
bracketpress.co.uk

John Paul wrote the intro to *Urine Mate*, and
Andrew Fearn contributed to *Showboat*.
Cock by Claire Williamson

Set in Linotype Avenir designed by Adrian Frutiger
Typesetting by Christian Brett

Printed and bound by TJ International Ltd.
Padstow Cornwall PL28 8RW

ISBN 978-0-9566184-8-1

1st edition, 2014
2nd edition, 2015 [two impressions]
3rd edition, 2017 [paperback]
2019 [2nd printing]

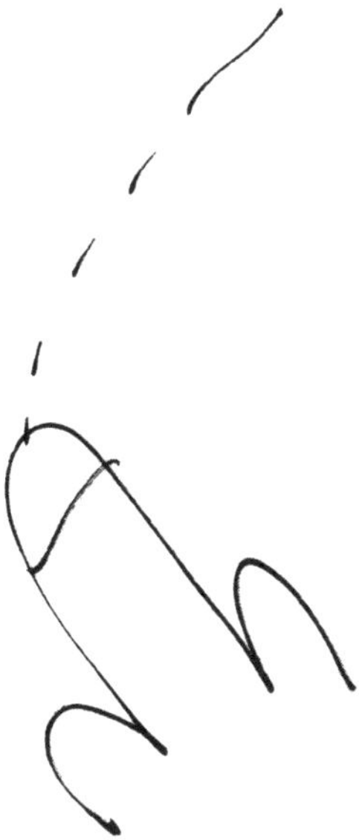

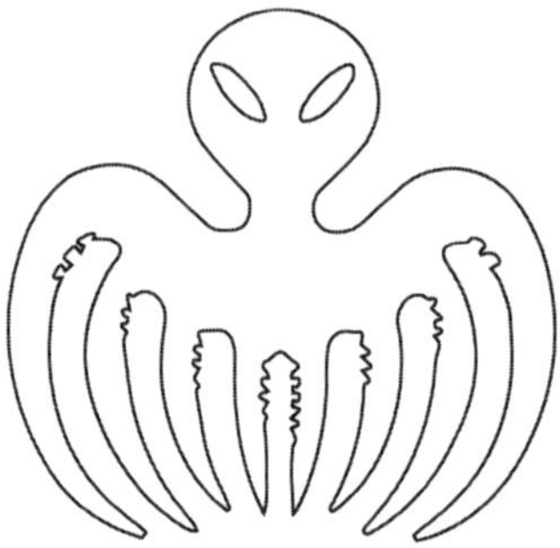

GRAMMAR WANKER

GRAMMAR WANKER

Sleaford Mods 2007–2014

Jason Williamson

Bracketpress
MMXIX

I'd like to thank my wife Claire for all of this. This book would not have been possible or the recent albums that have shifted the course of Sleaford Mods. They wouldn't have been possible because I would not have been in any fucking fit state at all to work them. She helped me, and I will never forget that. I love her and our children, without question.

I would also like to thank my mum and dad, who helped me on countless occasions and for nothing in return.

Further nods go out to
Andrew, Steve, Parf, Nat, Simon, Pieter, Nail
tons of others

Also by Jason Williamson

Slabs from Paradise (Amphetamine Sulphate, 2017)
Happy Days (Amphetamine Sulphate, 2018)

CONTENTS

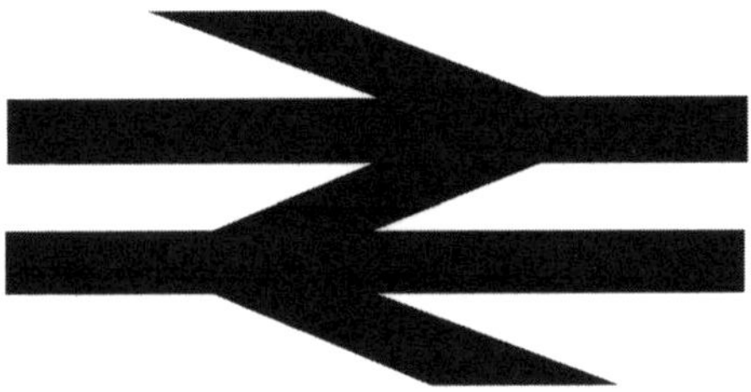

R&B PAUL

This is dedicated to the wankers that was
down from day one. More Mods.

Paul, what's wrong with R&B then mate?
Eh?

What's wrong with R&B Paul?
What's R&B done to you?
You're not a DJ
    you're a do what they say
I'll tell you what, let's all hang around the decks
Rinsing 'Screamadelica'
Rinsing Stevie Wonder
Rinsing Curtis Mayfield's 'Move On Up'
    well you fucked it up

Well, I'm well-up for reincarnation
    because this one's fucking shit
I'm the manager
I'm a dark bastard
    and I'll bum y'bird in a minute
    —*Alright?*
Dad's Army
Kasabian
and One True exploitation

it's a piss-take, y'posin' bastards
Launch parties
FHP's cheesy fucking photos with the token fit bird
    – who can't even suck my balls properly

    Let's build the brand up!
    Let's build the brand up!
    Let's build the brand up!
    Let's build the brand up!

Eh up, you've got some ug-duck in y'hair
prestigious retail outlets
y'got some ug-duck in y'hair
    —*What's up duck?*

Look at what you've done mate
a fucking horrible bunch of bodysnatchers
talkin' about 'Ham on Rye'
but completely missing the Catchers

Suicidal strippers on the night train to Gomarrah
    – I didn't fucking say that did I?
Bollocks to it
    —*Sod 'em all!*

Queens Med surgeons
Ketamine revival
Boring bastards discussing the merits of The Fall

Take the mask off
put that knife down
tell him to leave my guts alone Paul…
Paul?
Paul!

What's wrong with R&B Paul?
What's R&B done to you?
You're not a DJ
      you're a do what they say
I'll tell you what, let's all hang around the decks
Rinsing 'Screamadelica'
Rinsing Stevie Wonder
Rinsing Curtis Mayfield's 'Move On Up'
      well you fucked it up

Real singing mesters don't get anywhere
they pull their fucking hair out
they say things like, "What you goin' on about?"
and, "No mate, I can't get you any pills, I told you."
Chop your fucking face with a Les Paul karate kick
      smashing bar chord angles
Instantaneous… Brilliant… this is 'Tin Soldier'

—You look well J.
—What the fuck are you?
—A doctor.
—Well in that case I think I've got neurosis of

the shiver
it affects my long walk home
and all these tears coming from my eyes
my nose
and my dirty fucking ears

The master
of be dafter
the king of the other people's beers
Paul?

What's wrong with R&B Paul?
What's R&B done to you?
You're not a DJ
you're a do what they say
I'll tell you what, let's all hang around the decks
Rinsing 'Screamadelica'
Rinsing Stevie Wonder
Rinsing Curtis Mayfield's 'Move On Up'
well you fucked it up

Fucking stand here eyeing-up the usual slags
desperate housewives
desperate to do a bit of washing-up
hook an husband
get ya fucking purse out duck
the Sambuca Cartel

Impending angina destinies
the regret of fourteen years wasted
I cry my fucking eyes out
cos yesterday, I really miss my bastard yesterdays
Lob us one more
I'm a real raver
I don't know the score
Two – Nil
    —*Y'what?*
Two – Nil
    —*Y'what?*
Two – Nil
    —*Y'what?*
FUCK FOOTBALL!

Killing Notts culture!
Killing Notts culture!
Killing Notts culture!
Killing Notts culture!

GRAHAM

This is shit…
Fuckin' had it
    danced it
    necked it
    pilled it
    slagged it
    boozed it… it's all bollocks

Graham… play something sweeter
put yer drink down man
because there's nothing coming out
    of your left speaker
Graham… play something sweeter
put your drink down mate
I can't hear anything
    coming out of your left speaker

Loads of old people necking pills
ecstasy has truly taken its toll on some of these faces
the fucking eyes have hills
mine's wearing off
and the bird I've been chatting-up
is starting to look like a dead dog…
Oh, well…

Graham … play something sweeter
put yer drink down man
I can't hear anything coming out of your left speaker
Graham … play something sweeter
put yer drink down mate
I can't hear anything comin' out of your left speaker

Nottingham has defo gone downhill
this ain't the Kool Kat, defo ain't Venus
and why the fuck
    is everyone raving about Crazy Penis?
I got three women circling me like a hungry shark
only these ones don't bite – they fucking bark …
Oh, well …

I can't help but feel cynical
I can't help but feel bored
1990 came and went
I don't want it anymore
if I had the money, I'd go away
if I had the bollocks, I'd completely change
but my hens are caged, ain't free range
and I will rot in the shithole
gonna die of young age

Graham … play something sweeter
put yer drink down man
I can't hear anything coming out of your left speaker

Graham … play something sweeter
put yer drink down mate
I can't hear anything comin' out of your left speaker

Rottingham – where's Robin when we need him?
ain't giving to the poor anymore
he's selling to the rich
keep the foreign squad firmly fucked-up
slapped down in Fendi
dishing out Henry's at the side of the pitch
and on a three-day bender comedown
he smacked Little John with a hammer
he don't wear green he just smokes it *ma'an*
thinking he's fucking Tony Montana
– daft cunt

Graham … play something sweeter
put yer drink down man
because I can't hear anything
        coming out of your left speaker
Graham … play something sweeter
put yer drink down man
—*Leave him J.*
—Fuck off!
I can't hear anything coming out of your left speaker

Where's the fun
where's the want

where's the need
gone man – did one
been replaced by Satanists
who call themselves spiritualists
Boxsters
shit haircuts
down an' out greed
false prophets
dishing out twigs and seeds
"You want decent gear J? You come see me."
– bollocks
The path to enlightenment doesn't exist anymore
y'gotta get the bus
too many off licences
and too many bus stops
too many good deals on Special Brew
I'm in no fit state to talk to you
or God …
sorry

Graham … play something sweeter
put yer drink down man
because I can't hear anything
    coming out of your left speaker
Graham … play something sweeter
put yer drink down man
because I can't hear anything
    comin' out of your left speaker

This bean ain't working, sod it
I should have bought some cheese
all these cunts slagging me off for being a sniff head
now look at 'em
—*Yes please! Yes please!*
I should have bought some coke
when it starts getting desperate
any self-respecting timebomb is gonna take oat
I remember that bloke
he used to be a dancer – twat
now look at him, like the rest of us
stressing about mouth cancer – twat
stressing about mouth cancer – twat

Graham … play something sweeter
put yer drink down man
because I can't hear anything
    coming out of your left speaker
Graham … play something sweeter
put yer drink down man
because I can't hear anything
    coming out of your left speaker
—*J leave him.*
—Fuck off!
—*J leave him.*
—Fuck off! Pound on the door? Fuck off!
—*J leave him.*
—Fuck off!

SOME OF THESE PLANTS ARE BURNT

Some of these plants are burnt
but all of these plants are wet
you've done well darlin'
you've worked hard
it's been a struggle
but now you're all set

Rubber gloves ... what am I doin'?
Melton Mowbray, home of the pork pie
and now home to the demise of my
    Bank Holiday weekend
I could make a small fortune
    selling the crap on these scissors
I might need to have a number two on your loo
    if that's alright sister?
I think that was a little bit more information
    than she needed
But I'm too pissed
    and this is hardly a formal setting

Some of these plants are burnt
but all of these plants are wet
you've done well darlin'
you've worked hard
it's been a struggle
but now you're all set

The ride was nice, country lanes
    comfort, my bad brains
you can arseholes if you think I'm doin' this straight
    mate
I need some chisel
"Don't worry," he tells me, "It's comin."
Asda's doin' me head in
he's buying scissors, and I'm buying beer
four cans slip through my fingers and hit the floor
I'm pissed, and I stink
    it doesn't look good
so I calmly place them back and get another four
    La grande Stella
"You look like Paul Weller"
    —Fuck off!
The search for the truth
    has actually resulted in me living a lie
I haven't got a soul darlin'
    my fingers are mustard yellow
    and I never cry

Some of these plants are burnt
but all of these plants are wet
you've done well darlin'
you've worked hard
it's been a struggle
but now you're all set

She seems nice until she gets her phone out
Video phones are up there as one of the
    worst inventions ever
    I don't do bestiality babe.
    Put it away, and go get me another Stella.
    Please.

We finish up around six o'clock
but there's still lots to do
I know the chisel's coming
so I volunteer to finish it off
    —Alright mate, there's your thing
    —You alright on your own?
    —I've got to chip off
    —No problem
I've got four bags of smoke
a demo to listen to
a bit off that
do what you want man
    —Yeah, you fuck off!

At the end of a binge when you run out of everything
    your brain and your blood are draining
it's only then that you feel and think about
    the things that matter
the woman you still love
    that will never come back to you
a silent scream down a greasy pole

memories, love and pain
and prehistoric insects crawling out of every hole
bleeding noses
I want to be
I want to sound
as good as The Stone Roses

My teeth feel like chalk
I don't fancy the walk
so I'm kipping here
I'll get to sleep eventually
put a porno on
shotgun a load of beer

Some of these plants are burnt
but all of these plants are wet
you've done well darlin'
you've worked hard
it's been a struggle
but now you're all set
but now you're all set
but now you're all set
but now you're all set

MY MUSIC

I couldn't give a toss about your shit tunes
y'fat bastard, fuck you
game show host, thinks he's Quincy Jones
in reissue shell toes
close links with a sheep
they're everywhere
selling you expensive clothes
serving you drinks
or giving you a consultation
over ya flaky fashion hair

You are not obsessed with music
you are obsessed with the idea
of being obsessed with music
I think you're starting to lose it
Why don't you get on a Wham angle?
Choose Life
Don't choose music – my music
Don't choose music – my music
Don't choose music – my music

Countless promises
donkey's carrot
y'victories are few
this ain't Rome

you accuse people of trying to be mysterious
well, look at you
the monopoly isn't yours, it's a game anyone can play
I'll be throwing pint glasses at your bedroom window
when I'm doing lager shits on ya pretty Park Lane

Comic plaster, two black eyes
"What's happened to you?"
The Casino Kato
I don't need to be running around looking like
    Inspector Clouseau ... but I will
Any kind of trust, friendship – it will be walked over
I am a sex addict – it's a modern phenomenon
I'm a wanker – I'm shagging y'missus in a dirty flat
you hold the camera – get it closer
    because this is Ben Dover

You are not obsessed with music
you are obsessed with the idea
of being obsessed with music
I think you're starting to lose it
Why don't you get on a Wham angle?
Choose Life
Don't choose music – my music
Don't choose music – my music
Don't choose music – my music

There's no glory in beating down the door of
repetition
don't dress it up, buy a map
and brace your soul for the awful
unfolding scene of the future
bonafide recognition I'm getting hot-wires crossed
sheer frustration
why doesn't my key fit this fucking ignition
unemployment
stress
binges in dingy rooms in an unforgiving city
redeployment
only to find I much preferred
unemployment
and the feeling of you never know
what's gonna happen next
it's 34 degrees, I'm wearing a pair of crap shorts
and a seven-year-old vest
the exam went well
but I failed the pissing test
what a mess, what a fucking mess
more is less
because we are the Flatland Mods
in 1962 we kicked it off
and the West End jazz cafés got all the recognition
Phil Daniels didn't help matters
he should of had an accent from the East Midlands
the King's Road always gets the perks

but it don't work
like riding a P/X from Stanford all the way to Lisbon
I love ya Daz, come out of that dark patch
now let's rule Nottingham
they never even saw us comin'
because I sing loud'n'proud
for Black Gibson

ARMITAGE SHANKS

[No, I have no ambitions in that field, but I couldn't care less, I just get off doing what I do, and I do it very well. Thank you, I know. This is why I'm not tolerated. I can't be bothered to tell a lie. There has been something as revolutionary as the Sex Pistols: the ongoing force of ME ... and this you must never forget.] – John Lydon interview

Toilet Toilet Toilet
Toilet Toilet Toilet
Toilet Toilet Toilet
Toilet Toilet Toilet
Toilet Toilet Toilet
Toilet Toilet Toilet
Toilet Toilet Toilet
Toilet Toilet Toilet

I was wanking her off the other day and she was pulling a really strange face, these things happen in situations like this, so I carried on, made her cum all over the place. Then she tells me that she was imagining me to be a complete stranger. Well thanks a fucking lot, nice one. Luvverly. Next time then darlin' I'll tip up to yours wearing a mask, and a postman's uniform – leave the door unlocked – just bend over, and I'll shove it up your arse – throw a few letters on the floor – just for added effect. Bob's y'uncle, there's yer random sex.

Seven knackered fridges dumped on a piece of wasteland next to a house that's burning bridges with all its neighbours. Twenty-five kids sharing two rooms. Asda Smartprice. The bus stop's a youth club. Sovereign cigarettes and mushrooms.

Armitage Shanks   oi   toilet   toilet
Armitage Shanks   oi oi   toilet   toilet toilet toilet

Well, what are you sayin' bro?
Would you like a drink? I'll go!
I hear you're the toast of the town.
Can I kiss your arsehole?

You don't tell my bird you want to fuck her. Y'fucking leaving, Michael, you don't say nothin'. Sexual encounters like that take a while. She's got to get her head round the fact that you're a fat bastard with ginger hair – that's no offence to people with ginger hair – *but I wouldn't want it!* I'm sick of being talked down to by desperate blokes in Maharishi snow pants – that shit went down with Scaramanga.

WE
SALUTE
YOU!

Armitage Shanks   oi   toilet   toilet
Armitage Shanks   oi oi   toilet   toilet toilet toilet

Well, what are you sayin' bro?
Would you like a drink? I'll go!
I hear you're the toast of the town.
Can I kiss your arsehole?

Another do. I've been invited to that many dos over the last six months by people who didn't want to know me eight months ago – makes you sick. I wouldn't mind, but ninety-eight per cent of the music in this city is fucking shit. Armitage Shanks, a toilet fucking culture, and if you're not getting your arse shagged then you're the phantom bummer. You've heard it all before, you're gonna hear it all again, what d'you think I'm gonna sing about? My endless love? Ya fucking freak.

You won't have your looks forever,
and when they're gone ... what y'gonna do?
Give us a kiss. I can cook.
And look at the size of my tits!
I'd rather die in the gutter darlin', forget about it.

Ah, what ya do man when you're on your last legs and you haven't got a plan. The sheets have got blood stains. Bruises on ya thighs from shagging the wrong bird. Y'bed's surrounded by beer cans and empty chisel bags, mangled by your teeth trying to get into the fucking rock that's melting underneath. I'm a vampire. I've got homemade fangs. I make Shane MacGowan look like a cross between Joan Collins and Karl Lagerfeld, with his fan – messy fucker. Messy fucker! The state of your life, it's unstated mine. I've got oil on my ladder – it's on there all the time.

[Wayne Fontana, he did it.]

Livin' off your wits is just a toilet seat
Livin' off your wits is just a toilet seat
Livin' off your wits is just a toilet seat
Livin' off your wits is just a toilet seat
Livin' off your wits is just a toilet seat
Livin' off your wits is just a toilet seat
Livin' off your wits is just a toilet seat
Livin' off your wits is just a toilet seat

Armitage Shanks oi toilet toilet
Armitage Shanks oi oi toilet toilet toilet toilet
Armitage Shanks oi toilet toilet
Armitage Shanks oi oi toilet toilet toilet toilet
Livin' off your wits is just a toilet seat

DEAD CITIES

A pound in glass, y'know a pound don't last
pair of boots and leather uppers
united in the sense that they're both a pair of
    filthy fuckers
nineteen quid and that bird from Bulgaria wanted it
but I'm in love with you darlin'
—*it's a bit different*
the pole's the one, slide up and down
but it's not connected to the ceiling properly
makin' an horrible sound – I don't like her tits
I pause, and turn, drop another sambuca, two pints
the bouncer versus the Chelsea fans
pilled up, playing snooker
the loo's fucked, I need a shit
I don't wanna follow through a—
    ... bollocks to it!
—What's up?
—Here, just hold that will ya – just off to the loo again
—Why, what's up?
WHHAAAAAAAAAAAAAAH!!!!
—I've shit myself
    ... f'fuck's sake!
Dead cities
Dead cities
I'm gonna get filthed up

Dead cities
Dead cities

Ya can earn seventy quid on a Monday night
    sliding round a pole
In front of four or five rotting bits of bacon
    blokes that look like Dickie Davies
    smoking fags like it's the Seventies
Philip Morris' laid claim to every blocked up artery
    in this place …
    Philip mate, WE ARE YOURS!
    We are yours for the taking

Promote yourself darling, put that jar down
    y'fit enough, get a job in town
I'll have another drink, my eyes feel their way around
    this place is like the TARDIS
    it never settles down
Boarded up, it's blue paint
    I bet Stringfellas ain't
Russian birds like that advert on telly
    comin' at you in their hundreds
    and I'm the man for the job
Dead cities
Dead cities
I'm gonna get filthed up
Dead cities
Dead cities

I'm a ranting merchant
        slipping from the edge of a pint
while my feet balance on the emergence
        of a new form of music
these songs are shit and I'm gonna lose it
the multi-coloured lights dictate the tower's height
glass front town houses
where rich men pull birds from browsers
this is your modern day safari
Apple Mac corpses
let there be feeders
and catch the carvery
pick that cinnamon swirl up off the floor
shrink-wrap, germ-free, let's nick some more
rubber buses and the bridge works
strap-on city
I've done too much coke
—*fuck!*

There is no glory
and there is no hope
I live on Coronation Street
I don't need to watch it
Dead cities
Dead cities
I'm gonna get filthed up
Dead cities
Dead cities

THE MEKON

I've exhausted myself
I've exhausted myself
I've exhausted myself
I've exhausted myself
I've exhausted myself
I've exhausted myself
I'm knackered
I've exhausted myself
I've exhausted myself
I've exhausted myself

Who dares wins
Dan Dares
he got it wrong
his rocket got bombed
The Mekon
got a big head
with Sta-Prest waffle trousers
tram lines in his hair
a John Partridge shooters mack
fuck Lyle & Scott
the haves
      they always get it wrong
we don't
      we have not

I've got a barbed wire brain
on a cheap fight to self-destruction
with an overnight stay in —
I can't function
I'm not a mod – I'M GOD
I'm not a mod – I'M GOD

And you can stick this job
right up your arse

What's it like?
    Sticking probes into boxes of dead chickens
    until 8 o'clock at night
What's it like?
    Knowing you're just an average musician
    and this is your shite life
What's it like?
    Putting your cock inside another drunk woman
    — I'm like, 'Alright!'
What's it like?
What's it like?
What's it like?
What's it like?

She wants me to shag her
I ain't gonna shag her
– fuck her
I'm doing the can-can man

I'm a summer boy
I wear deck shoes with no socks
I feel wrong, I'm twisted
I'm a twat in a box
with no lid on top
and the spring's fucked
I hit women
I'm a bird beater
I guard my pathetic set of values
like a deluded social phobe with no friends
and a chronic obsession with becoming a Beefeater

What's it like?
    Sticking probes into boxes of dead chickens
    until 8 o'clock at night
What's it like?
    Knowing you're just an average musician
    and this is your shite life
What's it like?
    Putting your cock inside another drunk woman
    —I'm like, 'Alright!'
What's it like?
What's it like?
What's it like?
What's it like?
What's it like?
What's it like?
What's it like?
What's it like?

I stick my fingers up
    – well look at me
I do the pogo
    – it's in the city
I stick my fingers up
    – look at me
I do the pogo
    – it's in the city
What's it like?
What's it like?
What's it like?
What's it like?
What's it like?
What's it like?
What's it like?
What's it like?

STEVIE

Steve   Stevie
Steve   Stevie
Steve   Steve
buy me a drink, I'm fuckin' skint
Steve   Steve
buy me a drink, I'm fuckin' skint
— *Fuck that*

Steve   buy me a drink, I'm fuckin' skint
We need a bastard seat, sweet
Hey babe, get that one over there
        – *no, that one*
Hello mate, how are you?
I'm alright ta, how are you?
I'm alright ta
Yeah, he sits there every fuckin' night
        reading *The Independent*
Who's he tryin' to pull?
Janet Street-Porter?
He oughter
cos he ain't goin' to get anything else
        – the ugly little bastard

Steve   buy me a drink, I'm fuckin' skint
— *Fuck that*

Steve   buy me a drink, I'm fuckin' skint
—*Fuck that*

Y'can talk to me about your website designs
    all you like
you can tell me how much you'll push my music
    be a bit more pro-active
What? Like Flora?
Every tub looks the same
bunched up in a dud supermarket
that's just fuckin' lame
—*Friggin' lame!*

I walk around with me head up me arse
    knocking out tunes
    that people can only dream of writing
So you can come to me
    and if you don't
    – well fuck off then
There's always brown
    and dirty women
    in dirty juicers
    in a pointless town
Yeah, I'm Sir Lancelot
    and my lance is coming to a slot near you
—*y'fuckin' slag*

Steve   buy me a drink, I'm fuckin' skint
—*Fuck that*
Steve   buy me a drink, I'm fuckin' skint
—*Fuck that*
Stevie
Ste
Ste

TRIXIE

Da-da da daaaaa, da-da da daaaa
da-da da daaaa, da-da da daaaa, da-da bum!
da bum, da bum da bum
da da da daaa da da da da da…
Ba-ba-ba-ba-ba-bow
bow… bow bow

Flirtz… it's a dump
Half the girls look like George Dawes
    and the other half…
Biblical… Babylon
Primark culture
Leopard print tops
Suspenders
French knickers
Four-day benders
Groping pensioners…
I ain't being detrimental…
    I'm a tart too
… but we ain't on about me
    I'm talkin' about you

Trixie… what you gonna do?
    that double-ender, be the death of you
Trixie… what you gonna do?

that double-ender, be the death of you
    ... that's right

She dropped 25 anti-depressants
    and half a bottle of brandy
    before she left the flat tonight
Wobble wobble
Nod nod
You're up there babe
    —fuckin' God ...
She started in Leicester four years ago
Minimum wage – pointless
Career's – disposable
Prison – drink, drug addiction
I don't know bro, it's easy come innit?
    Y'know?

Planning her outfits – meticulous detail
Cans of cheap cider
and endless pills for the taking
Temazepam seduction
A relentless fuck machine
Give your lips a good shaking
Now you look like shit
    get a bath, y'stink
You look like Tina Turner
    tryin' to sell alcopops to kids

Inject some more ket
    shut up about your tits
Inject some more ket
    shut up about your tits

Trixie ... what you gonna do?
    that double-ender, be the death of you
Trixie ... what you gonna do?
    that double-ender, be the death of you

I got loads of lesbian stories ... do you want one? Did I tell you about the time I had to shag that bird? Well, not shag her. I got five-hundred quid for it. I done it for a favour – oh, don't ask. I done it for a friend ... a friend of a friend. Anyway, I arranged to meet this woman ... turned up at her house – I was a bit nervous, y'know ... didn't know what to expect. She come out the house, greeted me, and, I went in. I walked in ... and her husband was sat on one sofa ... on the other sofa was another bloke. I just stayed near the kitchen. She plied me with alcohol ... gave me a load of speed. She started kissing me ... it was fucking well horny. Anyway, she took me to the middle of the living room ... undressed me ... and just started fucking each other. Her husband was wanking, this other bloke was wanking ... it was fucking well horny. After about an hour, she went upstairs ... came back down with this double-ender – I'd never seen one before – I mean I was only eighteen. So we just got on it ... bouncing off each other ... it was fuckin' well horny. Then she went upstairs again with her husband ... this bloke came over – I was off me chops – really horny ... he started kissing me – I didn't shag him. I wouldn't, I wouldn't, I wouldn't. I got five-hundred quid for it. I was there for about three hours ... it was fuckin' well horny.

Trixie ... what you gonna do?
    that double-ender, be the death of you
Trixie ... what you gonna do?
    that double-ender, be the death of you

Inject some more ket
    shut up about your tits
Inject some more ket
    shut up about your tits

JASON STOP WANKING

["… y'so fuckin' lame, Jason. Stop wanking."]

I wanna get away from this Fred Perry bollocks
but I just can't adjust
I don't feel, I shatter
I'm a piece of junk
I'm made out of rust
And the shaking car won't start
in the dead grand canyon, dead grand canyon
The shaking car won't start
in the dead grand canyon, dead grand canyon
I just can't adjust
I just can't adjust
I just can't adjust
I just can't adjust

Cheryl Cole is a victim
but she don't know it yet
In five years' time when Ashley's
playing for Bournemouth
She'll be fucking Gary Barlow… and smoking glue
fucking Gary Barlow and smoking glue
fucking Gary Barlow and smoking glue
fucking Gary Barlow and smoking glue
fucking Gary Barlow and smoking glue!

FUCK ALL REALLEH

I'm sick of putting lolly on horses that don't run
and if I still owe you money
then you can wait for it you cunt
Yeah, things have moved on
I don't know where they're gone
running up the road with me fuckin' shoes on
And in the real world
I'm bloody sick of it
I'm a victim of myself 'cause
I never keep a lid on it
Ya all tin pot wankers
banging my ex on Spanish verandas
to the sounds of overground rappers
Kanye West is now finger fucking
Jo Guest
—*oooh, it only takes a minute mate*
And in the real world
I'm Gary Busey
throwing up food in restaurants
that shouldn't served me
it's Calypso mate
Montego Bay
I'm gonna fuckin' sit in the sun all day
cos I'm a fat reefer bitch
with a small dick

slim hips
my dick slips into any given hole
cos you know I've got dole … mateee, I'm tellin' ya

Get down on it, get down
get down on it, get down
get down on it, get down
get down on it, get down on it
get down on it, get down
get down on it, get down
get down on it, get down
get down on it, get down on it

And in the real world
I've had enough
I'm off to flog flats
in sunny Magaluf
instead of sitting in the house
and feeling dog rough
about fuck all realleh
about fuck all realleh

Fish fingers, chips and peas
I like eating bitch
hold on, I said, fish fingers, chips and peas
I like eating bitch
Get down on it, get down
get down on it, get down

get down on it, get down
get down on it, get down on it
get down on it, get down
get down on it, get down
get down on it, get down
get down on it, get down on it

CHEF'S OMELETTE

Hello, and welcome to Bleak Peter.
And here's one I made earlier…

Ronnie Biggs was doin' time
until he done a bunk
now he says he's seen the light
sold his soul to crunk
and I'm so fucking mortified
to think they'd celebrate
the death of a train conductor
when they smashed his fuckin' brain

Whoooooha, Chef's Omelette
Whoooooha, Chef's Omelette
Whoooooha, Chef's Omelette
Whoooooha, Chef's Omelette

Get behind me St. George
he was Turkish anyway
I batter my throat with fag smoke
I don't wanna sound like the bloke
from the Black Ghosts
cos I heard he thinks he's handsome
having a fag with Mel in *Ransom*

It might sound better if you didn't play
it might sound better when they get outside

Premier Travelodge
I don't mind, I'm shifting through the pornos
Premier Travelodge
I don't mind, I'm shifting through the pornos
Can I take this one?   No!
What about that one?   No!
What about them two?   No!

His girlfriend's laid in bed
with a quilt wrapped round her head
and I wanna look at her legs
but the quilt's wrapped round the bed
and we are higher than Jehovah
Jacky Danny I could fuck a toaster

> Look, I'll buy teabags.
> An' I'll give you what I owe next,
> at the end of the month,
> if that's alright?
> Can I take some of these films as well?
> No, I've gotta go an I.
> I know I owe you that.
> Oh, f'fucks sake, come on man.

Ronnie Biggs was doin' time
until he done a bunk
now he says he's seen the light
sold his soul to crunk
and I'm so fucking mortified
to think they'd celebrate
the death of a train conductor
when they smashed his fuckin' brain

Whoooooha, Chef's Omelette
Whoooooha, Chef's Omelette
Whoooooha, Chef's Omelette
Whoooooha, Chef's Omelette
Whoooooha, Chef's Omelette
Whoooooha, Chef's Omelette
Whoooooha, Chef's Omelette
Whoooooha, Chef's Omelette

CHOP CHOP CHOP

Chop chop chop chop
The demise of Planet X
Fuckin' bummers
—*fucking bummer!*

People Places Parties
People Places Parties
You don't wanna get me started
People Places Parties

I followed her upstairs
said a few nice words to her
then dragged her into what looked to be a
stockroom situated next to the girls' toilets
I picked her up
and placed her on top of two crates of champagne
unbuttoned her dress
and got down to some real Southampton
she said she couldn't give up on old habits
        – meaning me
which I though was sweet
but the last time I got off with her
was about ten years ago
you need to get out a bit more darlin'

People Places Parties
People Places Parties
You don't wanna get me started
People Places Parties

I asked a porn star if he was still doing films
he said, "Yeah," and if I was interested in raping
young girls on a fortnightly basis, then I should
send him a few naked photos to his email address:
sad twat
at
sad twat
dot cunt
dot cunt uk
so I went into the loo
got my phone out and took a picture of the
large shit fallin' out of my hairy fuckin' arse
I wiped my arse and
sprinkled the last few crumbs of stone into a roll-up
I walked up to the bouncer
lit it up ...
what's he gonna fuckin' do?
    – fuckin' beetroot head
I walk back into the club
a few nods
I seen the porn star dancin'
I walked up to him
I slammed m'phone right in his face

"Here's a fucking photograph you wanted.
Y'fuckin' rapist!"

People Places Parties
People Places Parties
You don't wanna get me started
People Places Parties

She insists I go meet her family for Christmas
at some crap twenty-first
in some shit club
so I went
it was terrible
bunch of thick bastards
eating cheap party food
she's bouncing around
flirtin' with everybody
jigging her knobbly knees to Jay-Z and Beyonce
        – disgusting fucking behaviour

I gotta drive
I'm eight times over the fuckin' limit
ne-nor nee-nor
I'm having to buy her dad drinks
        – that pissed me off
I bumped into some piece of wood in the bar
        – boring me shitless
with news that he works as a personal trainer

his ugly fucking mate stood there
grinning at me
if there's one thing I regret about that night
it's missing the opportunity
of filling that cunt's fucking face in

People Places Parties
People Places Parties
You don't wanna get me started
People Places Parties

[Skip, I got 'em, I need you to come pick me up, alright?
I got bit by a fuckin' diseased dog, Goddammit!]

I pick her up
she's got a kid
she sits in the front with her kid
the coppers stop us
I can't be arsed with it
we pick her kiddie chair up from her ex-husband's
he piles outside the house, screaming
scabs all over his fucking face
I can't be arsed with it
I put the kid in the back
tell it to fuckin' stop cryin'
I put some hip-hop on
the kid stops cryin' – weird
I drive

meet the geezer
he's horrible
horrible and hungry
we have to go to McDonald's
I waste half my burger cos his breath fuckin' stinks
he got rumbled two nights ago
so we have to drive an extra ten miles to pick-up
I drop him off
do a u-turn
wait for five minutes
then drive back
he's lost half of it
I do another u-turn
he's doin' his nut
        – I wanna hit the cunt
he gets out
he finds it
the kid's screamin'
eight ounces of flat crack
a fuckin' lorry's driven over it
this is fucking unbelievable
we drive
we stop
chop chop chop
a mini orgy
in the back of the car
the kid's screamin'
five different pairs of hands inside the bitch's bra

bitches brew
bitch's bra
one on

People Places Parties
People Places Parties
You don't wanna get me started
People Places Parties

North won't let me go
            North – go fuckin' left
Fuckin' North won't let me go
            where do we fuckin' go
The North won't let me go
            The North won't let me go
The North won't let me go
      One on

People Places Parties
People Places Parties
You don't wanna get me started
People Places Parties

CHAOS DOWN IN SOHO

Callin' all the coppers
    you need to get near me
there's chaos down in Soho
    can't you hear the screams
he fucked her in the toilets
    he fucked her in the club
he told me I was handsome
    he told me I looked good
so meet me down the Shadow Lounge
    bring some steel bars
I'm gonna smack the maggots
    and all the Johnny La's
I'm gonna crush the fairies
    and all the millionaires
the sugar daddies better run
    cos I don't fuckin' care

    Chaos down in Soho
    Chaos down in Soho
    Chaos down in Soho
    Where we are gonna be

Callin' all the judges
    you'd better get near me
I'll bring a darkness to your courtroom

and make your colleagues bleed
there's trouble down the West End
we'll hear the fuckers march
with steel bars and ketamine
and collars full of starch
you'd better find your jeep man
you'd better get inside
we slashed your tyres yesterday
there's no way you can hide
so burn the fuckin' motor
burn the man inside
lies lies lies lies
suicide

Chaos down in Soho
Chaos down in Soho
Chaos down in Soho
Where we are gonna be

THE CHERRY TREE

You don't love nobody
    no one loves you
If you go down the Cherry Tree
    they'll beat you black and blue
You don't like your aunty
    she don't like you
If she sees you down the Cherry Tree
    she'll beat you black and blue

Samantha
Sentence
The girls are comin' after you
You got a ticket to ride the snake
and now it slides all over you

Crack brown
brown crack
crack brown
—fuck that!

She nicked a monkey
cos she's a junkie
and now that swinging monkey swings off you
She couldn't hold it down
and if she ever goes in town

that monkey's gonna kick her teeth in too
        —*it's true*

She's a thieving little fucker
clucking harder than a crooker
and she sold her only daughter for twenty quid
She'll take yer down an alley
and you can tickle her Jack'n'Danny
A can of Fanta
that's full of piss
piss

                                                Crack brown
                                                brown crack
                                                crack brown
                                                                —*fuck that!*

Up Cherry Orchard
well where's y'starvin' daughters
don't blame y'fuckin' husband
he ain't there
He's beating up the Arabs in the shop
next to the garage
cos Samantha sucked 'em off for twenty Mayfair
        —*who cares!*

It's a shithole around here
where the fear breeds more fear

and the devil's got his prison well locked-down
Mr. Ferret, he's the warden
and he likes to bumfuck Jordan
'cos you'll never catch the man with his pants down

Brown crack
crack brown
brown crack
—*fuck that!*

SHELFLIFE

Irie
Yeah, you've smashed it mate

Well trendy

Mediocrity is in the city
    and there's a thousand words
    it wants to say to ya

Well trendy

Yeah, you've smashed it mate

SHELFLIFE

Wish I could go to another
    poor country in the sun
Shake hands with all the locals
    buy one of those multi-
    coloured frocks ... *lob it on*

SHELFLIFE

Proceed to pretend
    that I really like world music
Arrange a few gigs
    invite Damien Hirst and that
    other fat prick who's got
    an even fatter daughter
        ... fat bastard
To be honest with ya
    I ain't biased
    they both make me sick

Tracy Jacks, TRACY JACKS!

SHELFLIFE

Well trendy

You've smashed it mate

I'm currently wearing a trilby hat
– *on a slant* – sat behind
a Chas & Dave style piano
singing 'The Lambeth Walk'
with the bass player out of The Clash

Well trendy

You've smashed it mate

SHELFLIFE

Actin' all smug in E4 interviews
wi the bass player out of The Clash
good move
You've smashed it mate
... twat
I wish I had a drink problem
a Beach Boys haircut
moanin' to the *Daily Mirror* cos
you have to get up in a mornin'
and play yer guitar for lots of money
without a drink
FUCK OFF!
Try gettin' out of bed at four in
the mornin' with a crack problem
a cash problem

a real drink problem
Like everybody else
...fuckin' deal with it

Prostitutes on the stairway looking
at me like a mistreated cat
I can't do anything for ya darlin'
– *I'm sorry*
I smash walls down like
the Incredible Hulk
Then I'll just buy a pint and
forget about it
You can smell the wasted energy
in any pub you walk into
Blokes waitin' for death
with about £2.75 left
Nobody asked for this life
so don't fuckin' blame me if I'm
not livin' it right... *alright?*

Well trendy

You've smashed it mate

SHELFLIFE

Yeah

Wish I could put money into
people's bank accounts
Conduct intelligent conversation
thoughtful text messages

Mark, the only difference between you
    and me, is I have stuck my dick in it
Mark, I fed the monster
    and she fed mine
Y'don't even know me,
    and yet you pass judgement
    just because you want
    to stick your dick in it
You conduct intelligent
    bullshit, bullshit, bullshit, bullshit
Mark…
Oi, Mark…
Mark…
Mark?
SHUT YA MOUTH!

THE BRIDE OF RANKENSTEIN

Oi, Noisey... heavy fuckin' soul...

I'm nicking drinks off Vin Diesel
    and all his fuckin' crew
He likes to dance to 'Valerie'
    he hasn't got a clue
No more ecstasy... no more ecstasy

Boris and the Bride of Rankenstein have fucked off. I've got to meet her in the car park behind Next in half-hour. So, I'm in this fucking club, I keep takin' my coat off, puttin' the fucker back on, I'm fucking drugged up, I keep nicking drinks off Vin Diesel and his crew cos I can't be fuckin' bothering going to the fuckin' bank. She's half-hour late. I can have three for two or one for one, so I take six – fuck it. That's 40 pound which ain't bad, that'll do, yeah, ta. Get out the fuckin' car then. No petrol station's open, which means no porn mags, I got nothing at home so, I'll go Asda. I'm going to have to buy *FHM* or summat, *Loaded* or *Nuts*, full of tits. Tits everywhere, everywhere you look: tits. Fuckin' tits in the sky, big yellow tits beating down on me. I got a fuckin' tit tan, ma'an.

I'm nicking drinks off Vin Diesel
    and all his fuckin' crew
He likes to dance to 'Valerie'
    he hasn't got a clue
No more ecstasy… no more ecstasy

Y'robbin me blind ain't yer, you may as well be tryin' to run the charity box in the canteen at Scotland Yard mate. You got no chance. Everytime I come in here you shave another 20p off the purchase don't ya? I ain't stupid mate. It's cool though. I'm keeping count. In another two to three weeks I'm gonna walk in this fucking shithole and take four cans of Grolsch straight off the shelf and walk out. You owe me four quid blood, and if you try doing anything about that… I will kick your fucking face in.

I'm nicking drinks off Vin Diesel
    and all his fuckin' crew
He likes to dance to 'Valerie'
    he hasn't got a clue
No more ecstasy… no more ecstasy

But don't you want me, oh, why don't you want me
Oh, isn't it funny how they never talk about it
Don't you want me, oh, why don't you want me
Oh, ain't it funny how they never talk about it

TRAMP STAMPS AND TRENDY BOLLOCKS

Tramp stamps and trendy bollocks…
I went over to Morocco for the week
I ate loads of lamb and got munched out
with some weird shit and mange tout chops
are you surprised you flop? – I'm not
shocking bunch of opportunity knocks
Northerners ranting on about Pacha
you like the place so much
why the fuck did you spend 600 quid flying over here?
Tramp stamps and trendy bollocks…
Mondeo Drive
I won't repeat the fucker for a chorus
I'll just mention it once
I'm that fucking brilliant
I don't need to rely on gimmicks to write a song
too many tickling sticks on promises
and Ken Dodd's racking-up profit
I got money-go-round get fuckin' off it
and I'm not talking about that cappuccino kid shit
I'm a fuckin' coffee cobbler
so get it, slap it, fuckin' tit
did you see any of the ancient sites?
—*Did I fuck*
we stayed in the hotel and got grubbed up, duck
all-inclusive uncultured shit

culture's for pricks
sick pricks
like Silvio what'shisface and his army of
    extremely rich sex addicts
shoot the fucking lot of 'em
who orders a sculptor to carve the torso of Superman
    with their own head placed on top of it?
That's fuckin' thick
you're fuckin' thick, prick
Alley Beat – seven days of sunshine
laughing at all the swingers, cheesy bastards
you all real deadringers for love
all pop doves and grab the grannies
it's the return of the Jedi
Return of the fucking Jabba Fannies
Free drinks, free love, free entry, lemon entry
and can you fucking cook love?
Escort big'uns over 65s don't drink and drive
then why the fuck are you tryin' to sell me cider
with my half a tank of unleaded, Clive
I like the dive, rev it up, fuck it!
Middle England still wants to be a cowboy
on Route Sixty-
        —oh, fuck it
Tramp stamps and trendy bollocks
Tramp stamps and trendy bollocks
Tramp stamps and trendy bollocks

SWARFEGA

There's a man over there with yellow in his hair
    he thinks he's better than me
I'm gonna bang him out when there's no one about
    at the end of the shift on the end of line three

Doctor Spock
Vulcan Death Ray

I'm gonna burn his clock card
I don't give a shift shit
I try to get up but
    what the fuck for duck
There's nothing worth getting up for
Grey streets uneducate me
Slags knocking out
handjobs for discount

And money don't warm my bones
Devastate to liberate
The Concrete Jungle
Rainbow Bungle
Ironmonger's Legacy

Swarfega gets in the cracks
I've got green slime

I just need to

either

get a there   or die

Devastate to liberate
Devastate to liberate
Devastate to liberate
Devastate to liberate
Swarfega gets in the cracks
I've got green slime

I just need to

either

get a there   or die

Mr Big's a little twat with his Leicester crap
another side-splitting show
He don't represent me you cunt
fuck your Umbro
Burn it down to the ground
burn them Leicester man
fuck your Umbro
fuck your Umbro
fuck your Umbro

DOUBLE DIAMOND

These early mornings just fuck me up
smell of pale ale makes a man pale duck
I can't stand this fucking line anymore
shit galore
workhouse
and a knickerbocker glory
blocker
I don't like puddings
I'm dodging diamonds
on 16 revs per minute
it's a big cock faced bastard
and he's over the fucking limit
tomato sauce and some mushrooms
looks really dirty on my fucking plate
I got a fishbone hanging from my gob
like a matchstick mate
the yellow street light
unleaded
diesel
I start it up
pop goes the woo hoo
pop goes the weasel
the A52 Saturday nights' thriller
but without the chimpanzee and
tortured kiddie fiddler

I don't like puddings
I want a big bumhole to suck me up
"Who goes there?!"
It's Captain Cook from the planet
        —*I still don't know what the fuck*
          I'm on about duck
minimum cage
maximum cage
for me and you
minimum cage
maximum cage
eat it

Fucking drug dealers
after about a year
they start to lose weight
– sit down
not my fucking problem, mate
you seen 'em out and about
you can't have a laugh with these twats
just look at y'like you going on about something
you shouldn't be going on about
– what you gonna do?
why don't you go and get your main supplier
        over here then?
it won't take him five minutes
the fucking wanker only lives in St. Ann's
why don't you tell him I'm a prostitute

he'll come over then
in fact why don't you tell him I'm a prostitute
on crack
and that I'm willing
in fact, more than willing
to be his slave to wiggle and worm
through the rotten soil of Nowhereland
to live on scraps fed from the palm of his hand.
Go on get ya fuckin' man!
Chicken!

THE LAST THREE DIGITS...

"Ten ... twenty, thirty, forty – is that a twenty?
How long's he gonna be?"
"I ain't fucking ringing him again."
"It's him y'twat."
"I ain't fucking ringing him y'twat."
"I ain't fucking ringing—"
"—it's fuckin' him!"

Allistercandyflosshead
    y'bleach blonde twat
gimmie some of them Italian house vibes
    y'fuckin' birthday cake
you and that other posh bastard
    that Marcus twat?
How the fuck did he land a job at Rough Trade?
    Fuck me. The C.S.O.s are truly out ain't they?
No wonder artistic output in London collapsed
    with cunts like that at the helm
You're a fuckin rude cat
I remember tellin' the cunt a dirty joke in
    Brass Monkey one night
He just looked at me like Prince Charles does when
    he visits poor people in Glasgow
"Give us your money"
Pretentiousness is a bit like rock'n'roll:

you still get the odd cunt trying to hang onto it
the time for all that crap is done
it just needs to fuckin' fuck off!

The last three digits on the back of the card
Pauls'myth
The last three digits on the back of the card
Pauls'myth

Fuck the Kool Kat – a bunch of divorcees
tryin' to pull better lookin' birds than the one they've
dragged around town for the last ten years.
Fuckin' scumbags.

"Allistercandyflosshead would like to thank all the people that made the Kool Kat reunion a timely reminder of what a great party town Nottingham used to be – it's just a shame there was no young people there to witness it."

Of course there wasn't any young people there
you fuckin' piece of shit
Would you want to pay a tenner to spend five hours
at a fucking barn dance?
Allistercandyflosswanker
spin me some of that Pete Tong shit
DJ Headrush
— *ooooh! If you're looking for love!*
I'm sick of tryin' to hold it down

I just want to get fucked-up all the time
I wanna leave work
go pub
buy drugs
and fuckin' spit at people
  —*and you*
I like a bit of TV in the pub
the landlord put on *Unforgiven* the other night
  it made me mad
Plenty of them cunts in here
loads of Gene Hackmans
smirkin' over their fucking ploughmans
"Did you bring your lunch box home today?"
"Nah, I just left it under the desk, just put the fucking things in some silver foil will ya?"
Plastic fans for plastic bands
Shit clothing labels run by village idiots born with
  silver spoons in their mouths
It's all gone journey south round here
  —*oh dear*
Running across the road wi' yer fuckin' turn-ups on
nice chunky knit cardigan flapping in the wind
  another lifeless cunt running to the gym
I try to workout
I try to workout every day
I try to work out why I know more cunts than mates
  Mister 'I worked in New York for five years,
  now the company needs me back in the UK'

The last three digits on the back of the card
    Pauls'myth
The last three digits on the back of the card
    Pauls'myth
The last three digits on the back of the card
    Cheryl Cole – any hole's a goal
The last three digits on the back of the card
    Pauls'myth

I got a knackered tea-strainer
    swagging on Sainsbury's bleach
Last week a Romany had a pop at my girlfriend
    down the biscuit aisle
It's irreversible this dog shit
    and I'm slowing down
My intestine's a one big shit chute
    crayon brown
I smell like a fucking farm
a mad fucking farmer
giving a young calf his baby's arm. Mooo!
    —*Of course he's the fucking farmer!*
You're at the mercy of two men with more demons
    than a fuckin' Halloween party
Y'better count the colours in your Smartie tube
    —*job tit*
I turn my back for five minutes and everybody
    turns into Mr Blobby
Why you spend one-two-five quid on a polo shirt

— *it's shit*
you look like a fucking twat in it
You've settled for crap
You've settled for Plan B and
Ray Winstone's fucking daughter
Donkey Punch?
Just punch the cunt!
You've settled for RayBans and fucking Abracadabra

You get all tanked up, 'cause you don't let it all go
You get all tanked up, 'cause you don't let it all go
You get all tanked up, 'cause you don't let it all go
You get all tanked up, 'cause you don't let it all go

[if this world were mine …
I'll place at your feet …
… if this world were mine]

ROLLATRUC

[Nah son, let me tell these niggas something, God. I don't want niggas sounding like me … on no album! You know what I'm saying? For real cause I'mma approach a nigga man. For real man, I don't want nobody sounding like me man. For real son, you know. No doubt. Bad enough nigga, I don't want nobody sound like nobody from my Clan, man. Keep it real, get your own shit man, and be original.]

– Raekwon, *Only Built 4 Cuban Linx*

He said, "How many baskets did you put on
    that pallet?"
I said, "About twenty-eight."
He said, "Well I just counted fifteen, mate."

He said, "How many baskets did you put on
    that pallet?"
I said, "About twenty-eight."
He said, "Well I just counted fifteen, mate."
"Well that's because I'm not fucking interested — "
"What did you just say?"
"I said, 'what time's break Oli?'"
"Break's at seven o'clock
    – what shift are you from anyway?"
"I'm from shift one."

Cos this is what it's like, on the shop floor
when you don't believe in nothing

and you've got fuck all
This is what it's like, on the shop floor
when you don't believe in nothing
and you've got fuck all
I got a Rollatruc
I got a Rollatruc, look
I got a Rollatruc
I got a Rollatruc, look

He said, "How many pallets did you take off that lorry?"
"Fuck all Carl, cos I ain't had training for the forklift, plus the driver had to go – fucking lost it didn't he. Started throwing boxes against the wall, he wouldn't look at me ... fuckin' swearing his arse off at the fucking wall. I just stood there thinking, 'if he fucking touches me I'll bite a chunk out of his fucking face'. What a thick fucking cunt."
That's the trouble with people like me and you
we get stressed out about pallets and
fucking nothingness
cos that's all we got
We walk around all our fucking lives telling bosses
and anyone else to fuck off
Fist after fistfight after fight
until all we got left is a forty minute break
cos everybody's too scared to tell us
we're only allowed twenty

This is what it's like, on the shop floor
when you don't believe in nothing
and you've got fuck all
This is what it's like, on the shop floor
when you don't believe in nothing
and you've got fuck all
I got a Rollatruc
I got a Rollatruc, look
I got a Rollatruc
I got a Rollatruc, look

I fucking hate doin' music like this
    I can't fucking stand it
But I'm too long in the tooth
    to try and do anything else
I've had enough of these cunts in safe houses
    with popular music and all that shit
Wankers on the telly
    getting jiggy with it
What happens when the party finishes
    you happy bastards
Sob stories about how fame rescued you
    and your handicapped father
I'll break his other fucking leg
    Slick Boy
    Muscle Boy
    Entertainer

This is what it's like, on the shop floor
when you don't believe in nothing
and you've got fuck all
This is what it's like, on the shop floor
when you don't believe in nothing
and you've got fuck all
I got a Rollatruc
I got a Rollatruc, look
I got a Rollatruc
I got a Rollatruc, look
Spectre!

DON'T GIVE ME SILLY MOUTH

You get a little bit of power, made your job central
You hide behind the people, paying your bills
I know you got a cauliflower, I think it's really mental
To get it hour by hour, plasticine

Don't give me silly mouth – don't talk to me, I'm sound
Don't give me silly mouth – don't talk to me, I'm sound
Don't give me silly mouth – don't talk to me, I'm sound
... sound
... sound
... sound

You get a little bit of power, made your job central
You hide behind the people, paying your bills
I know you got a cauliflower, I think it's really mental
To get it hour by hour, plasticine

Don't give me silly mouth – don't talk to me, I'm sound
Don't give me silly mouth – don't talk to me, I'm sound
Don't give me silly mouth – don't talk to me, I'm sound
... sound
... sound
... sound

POLICE! STOP!

I think you're being choosy
put you on the spot
talk to me about tunes again
I'm gonna slap you in the gob

You got the thingy flowin'
you can hardly see the bar
you talk to me about tunes again
I'm gonna nick your f-ing car

Driving down the A15, with an aching in my heart
I do a ton in the 40 zone – do you wanna see me start?
Y'what?
Y'what?
Y'what?
Police! Stop!

Better not be cheesy
caught up in the past
horse shoe tunes, Mills and Boon
not working man

Well I knew you'd never get it
so I cut a long story short
assassination mate
drown in your own shite thought

Driving down the A15 with an aching in my heart
I do a ton in the 40 zone – do you wanna see me start?
Y'what?
Y'what?
Y'what?
Police! Stop!
Y'what?
Y'what?
Y'what?
Police! Stop!

Hubba-hubba get at it
get at it   brain down
Hubba-hubba
get it   brain down

Driving down the A15, with an aching in my heart
I do a ton in the 40 zone – do you wanna see me start?
—*fuck it*

Driving down the motorway tonight
    I'm gonna burn your tyres down tonight
Driving down the motorway tonight
    I'm gonna burn your tyres down tonight

MYSTERON

Save the fucker for later
Mysteron
Mysteron

Papers in the Moula
and people in the cabs
they all come out the Pleasure Dome
with loads of dirty cash
Land Cruisers made of chrome
d'you want a cup of tea?
they call me the Timbuktu man
I shoot down Lee Van Cleef
Mysteron
Mysteron
Mysteron

Jelly and the trifle
working on their tans
it's a front for sod all mate
cos you're the sod all man
the Bryant & May are comin' out
the card's behind the bar
they call me the Friday Special
the pina-co-la-dar
Mysteron

Mysteron
Mysteron
Mysteron

Right now do ya want to get mine?
if I had the chance I'd take it
all of the time
I beg you, will you take it – all mine
cos if I had the chance I'd take it all of the time

Papers in the Moula
and people in the cabs
they all come out the Pleasure Dome
with loads of dirty cash
Land Cruisers made of chrome
d'you want a cup of tea?
they call me the Timbuktu man
I shoot down Lee Van Cleef
Mysteron
Mysteron
Mysteron
I don't wanna be a Mysteron
I don't wanna be a Mysteron
I don't wanna be your Mysteron
I can't be one

URINE MATE, WELCOME TO THE CLUB

People, places, parties, J
you've already got me started, mate
'bout the cunts in the arm label coats
lookin' at me like they wanna slit me fuckin' throat
anyway, y'ain't got a clue, stop wearin' that in '92
makin' me on edge
wi' ya wedge
haircuts
don't call me gobby
t'you it's just a hobby
to use y'fists
anyway, I'm enjoyin' mesel'
your life ain't worth livin'
y'fuckin' prick
so leave me alone
an' get on with it
People, places, parties
inabit

Now just cos I look a bit different to you
handle it, and go back to y'crew
cos without 'em you're shit
one on one
cunt
handle it

Spectre!
I seen Roxy Rob put his bin out at nine o'clock
this mornin'
and all the people from Mapperley Park
point and laugh
cos he's pissed and he stinks of urine
You're in mate, welcome to the club
you get the private dancer with the ready-rub

I ain't successful either
fuck it, let's roll around in pig shit
hang around down Coral
watchin' the pimps kick seven barrels of shit
out the women
"Wha'hav I done to you?"
"Shut y'mouth and stand where I fuckin' tell y'to."
Two white, one dark
the only bookies in town where the horses bark
and vomit
the stench of El-Doctor
he dangles his victims from the legs of his helicopter
– fuckin' idiot
D'you think ridin' around on a BMX is gonna
make me feel intimidated?
Smash y'face cunt back into next week
along with the three snakes around y'babylon feet
You're in mate, welcome to the club
You're in mate, welcome to the club

You're in mate, welcome to the club
y'get the private dancer from the ready-rub

The only phone on the road is chlamydia ridden
    phlegm stank
where the fuckers sell processed peas as weed
it's cold when I look out of my window
another local pub burnt down to the ground
I fuckin' hate them Motown nights anyway
it's Jive Bunny meets Lucy fuckin' Pinder… on ice
I got a hoopla and I'm gonna fuckin' swing it at you
An' let's aim bombs at the licensee
let's aim bombs at the licensee
I rig one up to the toilet seat
I do a Lethal Weapon on the traitor
Yeah, I give his arse a chip tatter
"Yeah, ta-da."
You're in mate, welcome to the club
You're in mate, welcome to the club
You're in mate, welcome to the club
y'get the private dancer from the ready-rub

McFLURRY

Music for the masses
I'm outclassed here mate
in-between the 'taches
and splash out on shit
I'd better get a penny-farthing
and Marvellous Marvin
Slam-Dunk with a concrete record deal
it's bound to sink
under the blue rule
where the cuts make people stink
"You smell."
People look like emails
white smiles
shut down shops
couldn't walk the paper trails
an' in-house fightin'
gets the Tom, Dick and Harry smilin'
Boris Johnson and the Cheeky Girls
shut down the Underground
so it's back to orgies on the buses
"Drop us a fiver mate."
"No worries."
One pound twenty-nine on shag-all
McFlurry
McFlurry

McFlurry
McFlurry
I'm gonna wee in a basin
unleash an horrible lookin' vampire like James Mason
clip the ticket
the clip-it tick-tick
now let me through the fuckin' gate ya boring tit
what's wrong with this
it's all too much
Wobble wobble wobble
        I get out of it
Wobble wobble wobble
        I get out of it
Wobble wobble wobble
        I get out of it
McFlurry
McFlurry
McFlurry
McFlurry
I got a Brit Award
I got a Brit Award
I got a Brit Award
I got a Brit Award
No surrender
No surrender
Animal
five-day bender

MY JAMPANDY

Hate's a bit of a strong word as I bump into your sorry arse in the park, as I'm pushin' my little girl. But what else can you do when presented with a fuckin' idiot like you. I get a latte in the French style café and a croissant and jam. Sit down, try to fuckin' forget about it man. I hate that lad shit, that red top, "nice tits". That Ian McCulloch wide boy, bore me fuckless terrace bit. Long drawl and calculated hand movement. Has-bin. Silent partner at the back giving fuckin' blessings to up and comin' twats in macs. And your job made y'more confident, like a grub gettin' feathers and a beak. Y'got a big mouth. I fuckin' hate ya. Always avoid a cunt like you on the street.

The man is a wanker
The man is a wanker – he don't get much better
The man is a wanker
The man is a wanker – he don't get much better

Physically past it. Pasty Tax. D'you want a facial cavity courtesy of my jampandy? Y'fuckin' cunt. I'll have a thirty-two inch waist in raw denim and stick 'em in the freezer. Dunk. I got years on'yr, while you got belly on me. In a belly competition mate you'd win easily. Hands down. With a side profile matching that of fuckin'

Gordon Brown. Always at number ten. Always gettin' beaten by nine other men, ain't ya. Movin' up in the world doesn't mean using the lift mate.

"What floor d'ya want? Don't mind me – I'm in the fuckin' thing all day, eeeeeeeeeeee."

The man is a wanker
The man is a wanker – he don't get much better
The man is a wanker
The man is a wanker – he don't get much better

Torn apart in all the glory. Friendships established – y'fuckin' bore me. Shit wafer, shit ice cream, the ice cream man did time for obscene … behaviour. So why haven't you. Why haven't you suffered like you fuckin' should do? Boo-boo. Boo-hoo. Cryin' inside, sarcastic out front. Did I do something bad to you in a previous life you cunt? One on.

The man is a wanker
The man is a wanker – he don't get much better
The man is a wanker
The man is a wanker – he don't get much better
for you
for you
for you
for me
for you

FIZZY

The cunt with the gut and the Buzz Lightyear haircut
Callin' all the workers plebs
You better think about the future
You'd better think about ya neck
Y'better think about the shit hairdo ya got mate
I work my dreams off for two bits of ravioli
    and a warm bottle of Smirnoff
Under a manager that doesn't have a fucking clue
Do you want me to tell you what
    I think about you cunt?
I don't think that's a very good idea, do you?
Y'pot marked four-eyed shit fitted shirt
    white Converse and a taste for young girls
Don't send me home with a glint in my eye
I told my family about the fuckin' wage rise
    and got fucked on
Devoured, puked on and sucked up, ya fuckin' fly
Y'suction on your fly feet kept me pinned to
    the blinds
Whilst y'PA rattled out about emails
Workstation
Forced to engage in flirtatious conversation

Fizzy
Fizzy
Fizzy

Well just to keep the job
Just to keep fuck-all from turning into a
    fucking nothing blob
Bang it out
Go on, tell me what you really think
You got no chin – and you got no balls
    to chin 'em with
Glass panels separate you
The mid-price hand wash from the bin of used
    public toilet paper towels
We've run foul of the hidden hatred
    that festers in dogs like you
Tripwire
Talk that makes way for the vacuum
    y'piece of fuckin' shit
One on

Fizzy
Fizzy
Fizzy

Use a sheet of promise and the red shoes of Dorothy
    blanked out on a bed of thick monotony
With the usual stereotypes
    that fall for the lip
I fuckin' hate rockers
    fuck your rocker shit
Fuck your progressive side sleever tattoos

Umpa-Lumpa blow me down with a feather
      broken dagger bollick

Fizzy
Fizzy
Fizzy
Fizzy
Fizzy
Fizzy

DONKEY

Hold on, hold on
Bought rock'n'roll, what a con
Silly little leopard skins on
Les Paul singy-song-song
—*Nah*
Hold on, hold on
The dead streets walk nights' song
To the sound of the spit from my tongue
And the Ballroom Blitz went wrong

Revolution   Revolt   b p m
                        Revolt   and then
—*Nah*
Hold on, hold on
Hold on, hold on
Hold on, hold on
Hold on, hold on

Hold on, hold on
White collar bollocks singalong
Champagne vogue got us stung
Now the seaside donkeys don't run
—*Nah*
Hold on, hold on
The dead streets walk nights' song

To the sound of the spit from my tongue
And the Ballroom Blitz went wrong

Revolution   Revolt   b p m
                      Revolt   and then
—*Nah*
Hold on, hold on
Hold on, hold on
Hold on, hold on
Hold on, hold on
Donkey   Revolt   b p m
Donkey   Revolt   b p m
Donkey   Revolt   b p m
Donkey   Revolt   b p m
                                  b p m

PPO KISSING BEHINDS

Plenty people outside
    tellin' you that you don't need it
Plenty people outside
    tellin' you that you don't need it
But you will, and you do, and you always will
Plenty people outside
    tellin' you that you don't need it

I get the feelin' sometimes
I'd better watch how I speak my mind
There's plenty people outside … kissing behinds
You laugh at me, I don't care
I got all my greasy hair
I got a clueless idea
Killing me man

Plenty people outside
    tellin' you that you don't need it
Plenty people outside
    tellin' you that you don't need it
But you will, and you do, and you always will
Plenty people outside
    tellin' you that you don't need it

You fell out with the timing right
we got lost in the powdered night
we played dead cos we wanted to
now the life don't seem to notice you

Now the life don't seem to notice you
Now the life don't seem to notice you
I get the feelin' sometimes
I'd better watch how I speak my mind
There's plenty people outside … kissing behinds

Plenty people outside
    tellin' you that you don't need it
Plenty people outside
    tellin' you that you don't need it
But you will, and you do, and you always will
Plenty people outside
    tellin' you that you don't need it

SHIT STREETS RUNNY

I used to be a part of that door swings open,
      swagger to the bar crew
Saturday start at four, get fuckin' nailed down The Oak
      fly into the city in my technicolored dream coat
Stories told all night about a Rambo-style attack
      on any fuckin' arsehole in a sheep shagger's mac
I lived my life on an empty tank
      full of shaggy tit wank
                  Blankety Blank
And I always made sure the fuckin' contestants
      got it wrong
                  Bow! Bow!
I fill the frightening void with a chirpy attitude
      good as gold
I'm a nasty bastard in stage tights
And mate, I tread the boards and I'll bring the fuckin'
      curtain down with my uneducated hordes
I used to be shit streets runny
I used to be shit streets runny
I used to be shit streets runny
I used to be
Attention to detail
Attention to detail
Fuckin' email
WAV

mp3
I need a fuckin' bath
You ain't no roadrunner
You ain't no shoot shoot the runner
Shit take on it
Meanwhile, back at the crap cave
I trod on my cape by mistake
    and fell into the fridge, mate
I fuckin' hate Northern Soul
    it's like Motown's on the dole
And the Housing Benefit bouncers ain't happy
    with the inspection

Brian Eno, what the fuck does he know?
Doodling away with a fuckin' alien haircut mate
Head louse
I built a swimming pool in my living room
    and I called it 'Deep House'
You're so edgy mate
you're so edgy
Crap bands
I play to a crowd of no-one but have got loads
    of online fans
I'm cynical me, yeah, bitter
I post horrible messages to successful musicians
    on me smartphone … fuckin' Twitter

The dew on the grass in the park
        slap me round the face
I woke up
—*What the fuck you doin' in this place?*
It's not the wankers or the misplaced weaks
The fuckin' dodgy roofers, mate

THE WAGE DON'T FIT

Don't ask me to carry that cage
stay long hours
it don't fit the wage
minimal work it fits the arrangement
well sod extra sweat and out of town placements
cheap tricks
crap tattoos
and spotlight kids
put the till away
shop got ram raid mate
small
small
small talk about nothing at all
while you got a suntan
and I got what?
A piss pot
and we all get a free cream cake on a Friday
it's like school
with a bottle of full fat milk down ya throat
get them government anti-bodies
turn us all into young offenders
lifers and fuckin taxi drivers

When I said I didn't like it
that's because I really don't

I put the till away
get out the van, mate
we're gunna ram raid you
When I said I didn't like it
that's because I really don't
I put the till away
get out the van, mate
we're gunna ram raid you

The wage don't fit
The wage don't fit
The wage don't fit

You gotta be able to sell yaself
so I stuck my life on eBay – 25 pound mate!
Scratch the lager spot on my chin
I'm hungry
I'm worrying
I'm Tin Tin
I'm that dodgy sailor
I'm that sweat freak from The Kills
Jamie do me a fuckin' favour
banal banal banal
let down your long hair
what's in it for me?
A fuckin' ladder, it's serious
of course it fuckin' is
do you think I've ignored fame and fortune

for the fuckin' fun of it?
Smartprice Dicemen attitude
throw dice smart price
obscure no anthems round 'ere
just concrete chips a dirty sausage
a three pound bunch of flowers £62.79
I got fuckin' jumped! Wankers!
Concrete dagger swaggers
the glint from the blade
bounces off the ice arena
diarrhoea
night bus
confidence killer
your mug and my timing
it's dead
brick wood filler
wall plug driller killer
I wanna Bounty
"Well where's ya bastard Bountys!"

When I said I didn't like it
that's because I really don't
I put the till away
get out the van, mate
we're gunna ram raid you
When I said I didn't like it
that's because I really don't
I put the till away

get out the van, mate
we're gunna ram raid you

The wage don't fit
The wage don't fit
The wage don't fit

When I said I didn't like it
that's because I really don't

SHOWBOAT

Mine's a bitter if you want mate
Mine's a bitter everyday
I ain't a showboat... but you are
An' I'll die spittin' greenies in your face

I heard the rule was, 'Move to London'
I heard the monkeys get the train
I ain't a showboat... but you are
An' I'll die laughin' my tits off in your face

Showboat in the magazine
Showboat in a trendy fanzine
Showboat sez I ain't got a lot
Shut y'mouth mate, an' fuck off!

Cheap Keith Richards in your bellbottoms
An loads of models smokin' fags
I ain't a showboat... but you are
An' I'll die with these eyes over these bags

I heard the rule was, 'Move to London'
I heard the monkeys get the train
I ain't a showboat... but you are
An' I'll die laughin' my tits off in your face

Showboat in the magazine
Showboat in a trendy fanzine
Showboat sez I ain't got a lot
Shut y'mouth mate, an' fuck off!

Showboat in the magazine
Showboat in a trendy fanzine
Showboat sez I ain't got a lot
Shut y'mouth mate, an' fuck off!

DON'T WANNA DISCO OR TWO

[From a very large number of computer runs, making various assumptions, adopting various maxima/minima. There is in fact a general forecast of a breakdown of world society in the first decades of the next century.]

The entertainment for the night
watching a toilet swimmin' in piss
who's goin' to tip it over the edge?
Y'get a prize for it
People ripped to shreds by the whip of exploitation
deadened, bleeding, y'failed an expectation
I walk around lookin' at all the toe rags wi' no money
which one's gonna pop me
break into the house
nick the microwave
stab me in the throat
use my aftershave
Old Spice fucker
mediocre mediocre mediocre
yeah mate, I'm gonna blade ya
fuck The Maze
First Blood
I'll put a bit of wet dog shit in your hood
drug tits
scaly-faced booze pricks

no experience equals no deliverance
I'm gonna tip your canoe
copyist bollocks
we wanna get high
and we wanna get loaded
and then we gonna cry
and moan about the fucker

I don't wanna disco or two
I don't wanna disco or two

World Interiors and balti restaurants
Five Hill Food and Wine
eight pound on two pints
I got a fag off the barman
moody Friday
stop tryin' to show off
it doesn't matter where I got my coat from mate
"Y'what?"
—*Look, just fuck off!*
Rained stained callous
I want a pint and fight
I don't wanna improve my fuckin' life
for you
you make more money out of my existence than I do
I dodge the small towners
the music scene thick-they-ares
shit bands

you're all wankers
Grinderman bores
white funk snores
good relationships with the industry donkeys
who live down South
talent forecasts
shut y'mouth

I don't wanna disco or two
I don't wanna disco or two

Pukka Pies
meal deal with a drink
£5.99
pot-bellied promoters
cheap coasters
I can't get the fuckin' stain off
we know the song's shit
I like it, so what?
that's why I fuckin' wrote it
blasé, make ya clagnuts fight the loo roll mate
hey hey hay fever
Pete Wylie dog shit
singer turned DJs
fuckin' nonsense
just a quick quid
useless, like Ric Peet
slow death in Stone Island

alcohol
down the fuckin' Orange Tree
Strawberry Fields Forever
fuckin' what dogshit
Christmas log
jog on
Mystical Face Twat headlines
look at the wise men sing
I'm flash
here's the ball
I beat ya fuckin' soldiers up, Ming

I don't wanna disco or two
I don't wanna disco or two
I don't wanna disco or two
I don't wanna disco or two

FIVE POUND SIXTY

I left downtown in unwashed jeans
chewin' off his ear in the plastic screen
we race by mate, I got notes
I got a high-pitched chirping throat

Five pound sixty get me by
Five pound sixty don't know why
Five pound sixty past midnight
He could've charged me twice the price

Right back at ya
well, I heard rumours they get ___ed up
and I heard rumours they don't give a ___
an I heard rumours I ain't really arsed
well I'm pissed up mate, an he's got a car

Five pound sixty get me by
Five pound sixty don't know why
Five pound sixty past midnight
He could've charged me twice the price
Five pound sixty get me by
Five pound sixty don't know why
Five pound sixty past midnight
He could've charged me twice the price

Situations
when the sun goes down on the town at night
Situations

Situations
when the sun goes down on the town at night
Situations

Situations
when the sun goes down on the town at night
Situations

KILL IT CLEAN

We have to be, we have to be so small
We live our tiny lives, an' all we want to be is tall
We have to be, we have to be so small
We punch above our weight because
    the world won't take us all

The mouthy Mac man got a job on tellin' me
He's got his work cut out, so he better kill it clean
The mouthy Mac man got a job on tellin' me
He's got his work cut out, so he better kill it clean

Why d'all sound the same?
I came t'check it out
Why d'all sound the same?
I came t'check it out
I feel funky, I came t'check it out
Why d'all sound the same?
I came t'check it out

It stinks t'me, it stinks of all your pores
You got the bedtime stories
And I got the matchin' snores
It stinks to me, it stinks of high Heaven
You tried to pull a fast one, you pulled a clever'un

The mouthy Mac man got a job on tellin' me
He's got his work cut out, so he better kill it clean
The mouthy Mac man got a job on tellin' me
He's got his work cut out, so he better kill it clean

Why d'y'all sound the same?
I came t'check it out
Why d'y'all sound the same?
I feel funky, I came t'check it out
Why d'y'all sound the same?

Why d'y'all sound the same?
I came t'check it out
Why d'y'all sound the same?
I feel funky, I came t'check it out
Why d'y'all sound the same?

BORED TO BE WILD

I'm a tramp once more
easy to achieve
hard to undo
Little Jack Horner's been
sniffin' all the glue
and the pavement's back t'crap
It's the sound of a bus peddling
engine trouble
as it faces armafuckingedlin
It's hard enough, mate
sod the graft
I'm not gonna fuckin' spell it out for ya man

Bored nature
Adam's apple
loin cloth
Sod the drops
it'll eat you up 'til you ain't got a clue
about anything, mate
Dross fate
why did I fuckin' say that, mate?
what you on about man?
Jibber like a twat after a gig down the Caf
rubbing toothpaste between my fingers before
I hit the house

Spare room
    she's out cold
    oooh oooh ooh
He goes cross training
    she works out
    will they meet and have fuckin' unparalleled
        tantric sex

Bored to be wild
Bored to be wild
Bored to be wild
Bored to be wild

It's a grim life on the keyboards
    as the dead skin piles up under dirty inserts
    shift
Wild guns of Afghanistan
    800 feet up
    they can't touch me man
The Windsor Warrior taking insurgents out of the
    game – *what power!*
    "Bombs away, Ginger!"
    the royals never abuse it
Raggin' him in interviews for Lauren Laverne
    we've heard it all before
    for The Smiths fans on 6 Music – six what?
Six fucking ways to put people off
    there ain't nothing getting fixed with the State
        tool

put it back in your tool box, y'fuckin' idiot
the Golden Gates
the Seventies concrete, mate
hate

Bored to be wild
Bored to be wild
Bored to be wild
Bored to be wild

Salad dressing
logo restaurant
and clever partnership
A dining experience
that results in your fuckin' money
goin' in somebody else's sky rocket
Ripped-off with a promise of exotic dog shit
while you and your partner lick each other's
fuckin' face off
John Travolta
And You Will Know Us From The Trail of Dead
not fuckin' Mars Volta
Lots of darin'
lots of walls
that don't need to be fuckin' up anymore
landmines
what d'you fuckin' ask questions for all the time?
Smash the drill of a month on the wagon
only to be tricked by the wisdom of sobriety

ruinin’ my half-time piss
with delusions about being some kind of
menace to society

Bored to be wild
Bored to be wild
Bored to be wild
Bored to be wild

JOBSEEKER

"So Mr Williamson, what have you done in order to find gainful employment since your last signing on day?"

"Fuck all!"

Nineteen point four – top
Eighteen point six – middle
Nineteen point two – top
Eighteen point four, mate – middle

Jobseeker
can of Strongbow, I'm a mess
Desperately clutching onto a leaflet on depression
supplied to me by the NHS

It's anyone's guess how I got here
anyone's guess how I'll go
I suck on a roll-up, pull y'jeans up
Fuck off! I'm goin' home

Jobseeker
Jobseeker

"So Mr Williamson, what have you done in order to find gainful employment since your last signing on day?"

"Fuck all. I sat around the house wanking ... and

I wanna know why you don't serve coffee here. My signin' on time's supposed to be ten past eleven – it's now twelve o'clock – and some of you strange bastards need executin'."

"Mr Williamson, your employment history looks quite impressive. I'm looking at three managerial positions you've previously held with quite reputable companies. Isn't this something you'd like to go back to?"

"Nah. I'd just end up fuckin' robbin' the place. You got a till full of twenties lookin' at y'all day, well, I'm hardly gonna fuckin' bank it. I got drugs to take, and a mind to break."

Jobseeker
can of Strongbow, I'm a mess
Desperately clutching onto a leaflet on depression
supplied to me by the NHS

It's anyone's guess how I got here
anyone's guess how I'll go
I suck on a roll-up, pull y'jeans up
Fuck off! I'm goin' home

Jobseeker
Jobseeker
Jobseeker
Jobseeker
Jobseeker

14 DAY COURT

Hi dee hi, campers

Recognise the grief inside the failure of all that sends
the world to slime
Timex
Time Channel
X-Channel
let's ask the panel
phone-ins
wet dreams and sin-bins
drag your chin down the road
      as council paint cuts right through to the bone
television propaganda
is that all you got to say?
I don't care about the fact that you
      don't take drugs anymore mate
your attack is just that: attack!
It keeps y'dinner dates on the fridge you fuckin' twat!
your attack is fuckin' useless
your attack is fuckin' useless
your attack is fuckin' useless

Indie tours – y'can't beat 'em
like being 21 again, doin' pills at the Arboretum
linen army pants and no more numbers for

double dove re-orders
the desert landscape on Edwardian street corners
white paint like the rooftops of Athens
the good always shines through
as the people turn their back on the Golden Dawn
"I didn't get in to art school!"
an' still Vienna yawn at the legacy of Billy No Mates
the Iron Cross
and no, I don't masturbate
your attack is fuckin' useless
your attack is fuckin' useless
your attack is fuckin' useless

If you wrote that under a poster for one of my gigs
I'd be sick all over ya head, major
shootin' rats in the hotel bar
scene sharks
sit in The Rescue
utter cunts
artistic revenue
fuck off back t'your blood wedding Van Gogh
you got a fopp walk
and a cheesy passion for the fuckin' record store
Sonic Youth fan
m.b.v.
if you like feedback that much
get a job at the council
insignificant white twat with a 'tache

Nigel Mansell
rummmmmm, rummmmmm
hipster bastards git done soon
your attack is fuckin' useless
your attack is fuckin' useless
your attack is fuckin' useless

Yesteryear let's take it Back to Basics mate
Dave Beer
I said, I used to do drugs until I realised it was gear
L.A. Gear
I don't want white teeth and big tits
I want yellow fingers and missed mortgage payments
I'm in The Zoo
hangover
and somebody just thought I was Liam Gallagher
—*I'm not happy!*
your attack is fuckin' useless
your attack is fuckin' useless
I said, arrears one
        arrears two
        N.O.S.P.
        P.N.V.
        P.C.L.
        P.C.V.
14 day court
well, 14 day court
14 day court

BLACK MONDAY

Well gather your guards

Waitin' room
stench the loos
smells nice
faces of death rip the tickets
fifty potential health problems
cover the walls
I could have them all
who cares
death rays burnt the air conditioning
and smash out the warnings
that everyone needs to hear
this is the end of your cool Black Monday
deadly sixty
ray gun battered hate
I can't believe the rich still exist
let alone fuckin' rule the country, mate
dog waste
car showrooms
look fuckin' stupid
shiny inventions
unobtainable for the real
obtainable for the tits
big car

small life
that's just the way it is
Black Monday
Black Monday
Black Monday
Black Monday
Black Monday for the Tory

Well gather your guards

We took back the streets through the pot holes and
the last remainin' internet cafés on the boulevards
we over-turned world order
ten thousand strong
it's not enough anymore
just to have a fuckin' singalong
so I started hatin' the coppers
fuckin' show stoppers
low flyin' helicopters
spoil season five
nip tuck
cheap Weetabix
tastes like crab sticks
wake-up, what's that cunt doin' outside
near my fuckin' car? Look!
Echo Beach
glitter
Eighties segregation

so shit
financial ladder
false tit party
Blackadder
what has it come to when only the monsters
    point the finger
I'm not a burger
I'm not a fuckin' zinger
needles protect the neon logo from pigeon shit
and the blue sky's wasted
it's fucking sick of it
Black Monday
Black Monday
Black Monday
Black Monday
Black Monday for the Tory
Black Monday
Black Monday
Black Monday
Black Monday
Black Monday
Black Monday
Black Monday
Black Monday
Black Monday

JOLLY FUCKER

Promote y'self
look like a cunt
Vodka parties
cushioned walls in a shit club
I ain't bothered where it goes
I got a job
I rot away in the aisles at the Co-op mate
no prob
French Fancies
Mr. Kipling acid dances
let's laugh at local record plants
elitist hippies
arrogant cunts
Ian Beale tight trunks
tight pants
grammar wanker
walk the plank
pirate manky
sixty kids – where's mine?
wastin' money on shit coffee all the time
fish fingers
take the batter off
I can't believe you had kids
—*Fuck off!*

Jolly Fucker
Jolly Fucker
Jolly Fucker
Mister Jolly Fucker

Lamplight boogie
re-press re-press
bus cunt
move then mate
move for fuck’s sake
the machine don’t bleep
ticketless
sheep
bah-bah crack sheep
have you any rock
E.D.L. twat
Tommy used to work on the dock
union went all white
– he fuckin’ loved it
take it down there
take it down there
camouflage
Humpty Dumpty
Crusades
blood on the hands of working class rage

Jolly Fucker
Jolly Fucker

Jolly Fucker
Mister Jolly Fucker

Why do I walk on City and Guilded splinters
digital time boards are the new public shitters
soft dips in hard roads
curry night
I'd better watch my words
two-pint buzz
and loads of office turds
push in
don't push me
I was here first you cunt
can't you fuckin' see?

Jolly Fucker
Jolly Fucker
Jolly Fucker
Mister Jolly Fucker

TWEET TWEET TWEET

I get a shaky start to Tuesday
sweat stains on bus windows
I don't wanna ruin my coat but
that's just the way it goes
"Cheer up you fuckin' bastard."
that's all I heard him say
St. George's flag on white van
this is the human race

This is the human race
UKIP and your disgrace
chopped heads on London streets
all you zombies tweet tweet tweet
this is the human race
UKIP and your disgrace
chopped heads on London streets
all you zombies tweet tweet tweet

These wheels are turning tricks
this bus is full of pricks
eight hours of Gedling council
fuck your life it's spare room hassle
dead weight is living flesh
we are no longer spesh
these grips that pull my hair
a life not lived cos I don't care

This is the human race
UKIP and your disgrace
job tits on London streets
all you zombies tweet tweet tweet
this is the human race
UKIP and your disgrace
job tits on London streets
all you zombies tweet tweet tweet

Well I just bit half of mine
throw myself on the Metroline
when I walk back from the train
with a Stella kicking in my brain
well I just bit half of mine
throw myself on the Metroline
when I walk back from the train
with a Stella kicking in my brain

BAMBI

This song's about drones and water cannons
One. Two. Three. Four!

What ya tellin' people ya old for?
are you that bothered about it?
you're in the pop star market
"Oh yea, I forgot..."
ya big mates used to skate
Thrasher Magazine
"Oh yea, I forgot..."
"Oh yea, I forgot..."
Commercial Road
ya never gettin' off it
you play gigs like Kurt Cobain
"Oh yea, I forgot..."
"Oh yea, I forgot..."
you play gigs like Kurt Cobain
"Oh yea, I forgot..."
Fuck off posey pants, rock toss
you're in the pop star market
sexy promoters, untouchable organisations
"Oh yea, I forgot..."
"Oh yea, I forgot..."
"Oh yea, I forgot..."
"Oh yea, I forgot..."

Sexy QE2 like quiz night at the I Puke On You Inn
minge twat, quim quim quim
die like a raisin face like
Alvin Stardust did black leather
                    black leather
Steve Jones, Eighties didn't work out
but at least you did a tune wi fuckin' Axl Rose
minge twat, quiz night, bang bang bang
who killed Bambi, man
who killed Bambi, man   "Oh yea, I forgot..."
who killed Bambi, man   "Oh yea, I forgot..."
who killed Bambi, man   "Oh yea, I forgot..."
                               "Oh yea, I forgot..."

SCENERY

The wet soaks the building halfway down
it's all I can see apart from the fuckin' car park
bags on eyes from debts and cries of help
down the funnel of fucking nothing
policy still applies
No mate, you can cry
for those chopped down in interview rooms
the Rolls Royce engine of tax still looms
and doesn't give a toss about your fucking cancer
sunbeds half price at the end of the till
an shit staff shuffle
they all look really ill
I'll be the first generation to take
        a real drop in living standards
candlelight bastards
Tiny Tim chancers
snowflakes lay on Georgian windows
        in small walkways

Scenery
Scenery
Scenery

Cheap office gags
airport sweets

No milk
"Well, I ain't fuckin' buyin' any!"
Cheap midget gems
my teeth get violent fems
and laugh at the thought of shit tattoos
I sell booze from the back of a van like a sad cunt
with crap ideas about clearin' arrears
a big tickle
crap chippy
fuckin' head gone pickle
the red curtain of wankers
wanker and sickle
and ride an horse with no top on
no wonder ya churches are gettin' played out
by virtually everyone

Scenery
Scenery
Scenery

Cutter's Choice
who's choice?
the trees turn into twigs that jump on my lips
hello mate, we're cigs
get used to it
get laid out on a grey stretch of road
Saino's
Fosters

cos I'm gettin' fuckin' old
rooftops kiss the arboretums
two fingers firmly up at the Range Rover
thick cunt billionaires
up'n'down the hill
Aye, big boy
who fuckin' cares

Scenery
Scenery
Scenery
Scenery
Scenery
Scenery
Scenery

ROUTINE DEAN

Westgate
I waited until he walked out and double-turned
near the bank to walk back round
sending me on a wild goose chase
fillin' in forms
upstairs downstairs
little details
nobody gives a fuck
who cares
left with a cola-cube full of boundless rage
slip and limp into the next but the feeling still remains

I hate what you do and I don't like you
I hate what you do and I don't like you

Barriers that need your ticket number
the queue gathers length
I used it as a fucking toothpick
waitin' on the chair near ward eight
I'm a swivel servant
years of service mate
I'll piss in a cup and throw at y'boss
golden handshake
profile people
living as profile page pixels
match the info section to match your broad range

I hate what you do and I don't like you
I hate what you do and I don't like you
I hate what you do and I don't like you

Routine Dean so do I
it's like biting bricks and a dead eye
struggle of work
day is dressed down naïvety
and deep frowns and long days
I go crazed
no life gives
no like makes
cocooning
mobility's gonna move me
I pick up the phone
I'm already there
but I didn't even fuckin' feel the journey
the private bubble
no you and me
just that electracide electricity

I hate what you do and I don't like you
I hate what you do and I don't like you
I hate what you do and I don't like you
I hate what you do and I don't like you
I hate what you do and I don't like you
I hate what you do and I don't like you

PUBIC HAIR LTD.

Why you fuckin' hidin', behind the stupid car
doin' 30 in a 40, playin' solo Johnny Marr

Who gives a fuck about yesterday's heroes
Who seem to think that they are still today's heroes
It's not a pyramid – y'not a fucking pharaoh

Sick of all these pissy sell-outs, ignoring actuality
that everything that made them great, lost its validity

Who gives a fuck about yesterday's heroes
Who seem to think that they are still today's heroes
It's not a pyramid – y'not a fucking pharaoh

Pubic Hair Limited
Pubic Hair Limited
Pubic Hair Limited
Pubic Hair Limited
Pubic Hair Limited
Pubic Hair Limited
Pubic Hair Limited
Pubic Hair Limited
Pubic Hair Limited

Why you fuckin' hidin', behind the stupid car
doin' 40 in a 30, playin' solo Johnny Marr

Who gives a fuck about yesterday's heroes
Who seem to think that they are still today's heroes
It's not a pyramid – y'not a fucking pharaoh

Sick of all these pissy sell-outs, ignoring actuality
that everything that made them great, lost its validity

Who gives a fuck about yesterday's heroes
Who seem to think that they are still today's heroes
It's not a pyramid – y'not a fucking pharaoh

Pubic Hair Limited
Pubic Hair Limited
Pubic Hair Limited
Pubic Hair Limited
Pubic Hair Limited
Pubic Hair Limited
Pubic Hair Limited
Pubic Hair Limited
Pubic Hair Limited

AIR CONDITIONING

Alright, alright...
Waitin' room stench
the loo's smell nice
faces of death rip the tickets
50 potential health problems
cover the walls
I could have them all
—who cares

Death rays burn the air conditioning
Death rays burn the air conditioning
Death rays burn the air conditioning
Death rays burn the air conditioning

Alright, alright...
Death rays burn the air conditioning
and smash out the warnings
that everyone needs to hear
this is the end
this is the end of your cool
Black Monday

Deadly 60
Ray gun battered hate
I can't believe the rich still exist
let alone run the fuckin' country, mate

Death rays burn the air conditioning
Death rays burn the air conditioning
Death rays burn the air conditioning
Death rays burn the air conditioning

Alright, alright …
Dog waste car showroom
look fuckin' stupid, shiny
inventions unobtainable
for the real
obtainable for the tits
big car, small life
that's just the way it is
I been debt and confused
for so long it's not true

Death rays burn the air conditioning
Death rays burn the air conditioning
Death rays burn the air conditioning
Death rays burn the air conditioning

TIED UP IN NOTTZ

The smell of piss is so strong
    it smells like decent bacon
Kevin's gettin' footloose on the overspill
under the piss station
two pints destroyer
on the cobbled floors
no amount of whatever is gunna chirp the chip up
it's the Final Countdown by fucking Journey
I woke up with shit in my sock
outside the Polish off licence
"They don't mind," said the arsehole to the legs
you gotta be cruel to be kind
shit bank save it up like Norbert Colon
release the stench of shit grub
like a giant toilet kraken
the lonely life that is touring
I got an armful of decent tunes mate
but it's all so fucking boring

Tied up in Nottz
With a Z you cunt
Black t-shirts and State toss
Nobby's Nuts the rule of Rough Cutz
A to Z of nothing gets all the shiz
We are real

we are lookin' 20p and the 10p mix
crab eyes another lonely little DJ with no fuckin' life
Weetabix England fuckin' Shredded Wheat
Kellogg's cunts on bleak shiz art cock
the green light don't stop the shit
homegrown dealers of Berlin beggin' for lolly and
it's beautiful how the privileged still let 'em in

Tied up in Nottz
Shit, and the dealers tipped up
Tied up in Nottz
Shit, and the dealers tipped up

A LITTLE DITTY

Cat pepper
we been told what to do
I didn't realise either mate
I'm with you
I been following white lines all my life
Touché Turtle
jump the castle
avoid the disco dancers
no hassle
doing beak like that with a kid at your mum's
paramedics
ya should've thought about that one
heart stopper
BOOM!   CLEAR!
What happened to Richard?
all I can see is gear
breathless
incinerate
processed cheese
become what you hate
become what we are
a Series One with dreams to reach a Series Four
drive drive
six packs
drive drive

white teeth KitKat
take the money and run
join the elite
you sold yaself to no-one
Pied Piper
whisky nose
the Wonderwall fell down on you

A little ditty and it's all gone wrong
I don't expect the tool to sing along
A little ditty and it's all gone wrong
A little ditty
A little ditty

I ain't a threat
they leave me alone
flat cut gamble
yer know when I worked there
I got a bad feelin' from the man
I can't work wi someone like that again san
A little ditty and it's all gone wrong
I don't expect the kid to sing along
That band from the '80s, that punk band
what are they called, the Queens Park Rangers?
        – been around ages you tool
We all up in the top room of the pub
getting heavy with the past that didn't exist
you re-shape to get celeb mates

Shoreditch yarn
in the have you been for a poo poo barn
narly coke death faces
death death death
nine to a cubicle
death beds
wheezing screwing up faces
last choke push the wheels of the next big thing
you scratch my back
I don't scratch anything
apart from my nads
Oi Mick!
I'm born to be bland
chubbed up in black leather
Flint's death currywurst
smashed and in everything

A little ditty and it's all gone wrong
I don't expect the tool to sing along
A little ditty and it's all gone wrong
A little ditty
A little ditty

YOU'RE BRAVE

Sat around the bloke's house
he liked me cos I made some informed comment
about the early history of his fuckin' country
big mirror, lumps of drugs, his own private lift
shit pieces of art
matter of fact statements about
how he's pickin' his kids up in two hours
twat
as if
You're brave
You're brave
You're brave

Yeah, ain't we all
chain smoke ya fags
I ain't listenin' t'you mate
I ain't listenin' to fuck all
I just wanked in ya toilet
polish that you connoisseur
I'm a connoisseur
I've conned you sir
nick ya biscuits
laugh
we ya mates
wanked in ya toilet

you fuckin' tit rifle
yawn
turn this wannabe inner city angst shit off
you're in the presence of toiletry
from under the rim
drips the bleach thing
mmmmmmmaawwwwwwah
horrible strands of brown waste
brown lace
Nottz lol
You're brave
You're brave
You're brave

I'm gettin' weird looks from his girlfriend
what did she expect?
the parlour's alright
it's a nice city
but I'm tired
wrecked
bored
I've lived ten thousand lives
more than these kids in wonderland
when it turns black then the realisation
will change that party face
you gotta change ya friends
who love you long time, lol
chicken mix, large, no salad, open

times two
I wanna place like this
how do I get it?
it's beautiful
it's fuckin' ridiculous
how d'you spell that?
Chumbawamba weren't political
    they were just crap
You're brave
You're brave
You're brave
Oh ain't we brave
oh ain't we brave
oh ain't we all just pissing
in the flames

You're just pissing in the flames
Oh, ain't we brave

STRIKE FORCE

The corner wakes everybody up
especially the 'me first' waitin' to jump
midnight snipers
prowlin' the shopping centre whilst it's quiet
whilst the flowerman sets up
braggin' about the money he's got
the petite bourgeoisie with his new van
an' fuckin plantin' pots
brown plastic
the man always acts fantastic
Tesco Extra an a real bad cough
that stinks of microwaved rice with beef stroganoff

The struggle in words   swivel servant
The struggle in words   swivel servant

The war torn lino on the toilet floor
and the way the decorator's mate blends it all in
we are caged
tryin' to pick preferences out the unlucky bin
strangers grunt and make a mess near the fuckin' sink
tuck my shirt in
shrunk from too much washin'
twenty quid y'get what you give
an' I'm not talkin' 'bout that twat either

the wind blows on the favoured
who managed to grease the eager machine
eager beaver

The struggle in words civil servant
The struggle in words swivel servant
Adjust my tie, I hate this lie
The struggle in words swivel servant

I can't see it
ranges from "Pick your nose and do something else"
to "I just can't fuckin' believe it"
can't you like it or can't you like it
The Club of Rome holds two grapes
and they belong to me mate
I got the option to cycle and get fit
get the bus
taxi
walk it
roundabouts
cogs
blocked
Audi T4
some twat on a fix
everybody looks like they got it
The strugglin' words swivel servant
The strugglin' words swivel servant
Adjust my tie I hate this lie

The strugglin' words   swivel servant
Adjust my tie   I hate this lie
Adjust my tie   I hate this lie
Adjust my tie   I hate this lie
The strugglin' words
Strike Force
Strike Force
Strike Force
Strike Force
Strike Force
Strike Force
Strike Force
Strike Force

THE CORGI

The corgi – the Palace gets it right
The corgi – it's always warm at night
The corgi – the driveway and the range
The corgi

Mighty old times where will we be
trench foot horror they overtake me
the yellow mist falls, oh what we gonna do
history repeats like BBC2

The corgi – the Palace gets it right
The corgi – it's always warm at night
The corgi – the driveway and the range
The corgi

To make it obscure is the mark of a man
live a life of freedom near the river in France
I ain't no mouthy baker, the cake ain't for me
a four pint punter in the Chinese

The corgi – the Palace gets it right
The corgi – it's always warm at night
The corgi – the driveway and the range
The corgi

The guns ain't gonna scream
no signs of rain, no signs of rain
let's walk it down
The guns ain't gonna scream
no signs of rain, no signs of rain
let's walk it down
The men ain't gonna scream
no signs of pain, no signs of pain
lets walk it down
The men ain't gonna scream
no signs of pain, no signs of pain
no signs of pain

The corgi – the Palace gets it right
The corgi – it's always warm at night
The corgi – the driveway and the range
The corgi

FROM RAGS TO RICHARDS

The fame … the fame
What else you got apart from chipboard
and Sir Lancelot
fags and meat
Lincolnshire tweets
get slick, we mean it
kitchens and sniff
go hand in hand
like the wankers it employs
sexy people in shiny shit
with bags of it
to enjoy
have a bit of realism
no teeth and a bus stop seat
that's your house
y'racy prick
the tedium that connects itself to the nibble
local media
and posh suburban wankers
live in Brussels

From rags to Richards
the ferry got us out of the pain
From rags to Richards
I hope I don't see that daft cunt again

Blocked off
the entrance to this flat
and that
the life of a band
attracts the chubbs in packs
chubbed up mate
it's sex shows on tap
Heaven 17
is that the house, name and number, Pat?
Rick got slick on a dark hole man
missed his train
—*Did he fuck!*
he didn't even go to the station duck
grey walls that tower
old bricks
stop the car Pete, I'm gonna be sick
spray gun
make the petrol stain flowers wish they had done
parlour tales of death threats on golden thrones
those cunts at the top
carry hollow bones in throws
Findus crispy human fingers
Captain Sadist
hundred per cent cod
—*Fuck off!*

From rags to Richards
the ferry got us out of the pain

From rags to Richards
I hope I don't see that daft cunt again
The fame ... the fame
Look mate, we got to get together
—*What for?*
motorbikes kiss the green lights
snore snore snore
Look mate, we got to get together
—*What for?*
motorbikes kiss the green lights
snore snore snore
The fame ...
The fame ...
The fame ...
The fame ...
The fame
The fame
The fame
The fame
The fame
The fame
The fame
The fame
The fame
The fame
The fame
The fame
The

LIVEABLE SHIT

So, I got in this mornin'
and I went to the loo
and he walked out of a cubicle
and it fuckin' stunk
every mornin' I get in an it's the
same time, same traps, same stink
and it glides through the air
by the time it's hit yer
it's been pacified by ten yards of fresh air
Liveable shit – you put up with it
Liveable shit – you put up with it

And the narly fuckin' arseholes that gather
no balls to do anything apart from sliver
mixed in with knowledge and no localism
just fake accents nicked from someone posh
they might have met at Shoreditch
a vegetarian vet
Lou fuckin' Reed
whoever
G.G. fuckin' Allin
gestures of violence to anybody
who can't see or hear them
that kind of prick
that kind of shit

Liveable shit
like three months of rain
nobody likes a fuckin' Tory reign
the Prime Minister's face hangin' in the clouds
like Gary Oldman's Dracula
as Keanu Reeves drives up to the fuckin' castle
laughin' really badly
relentless
like the gears on a bus if you're sat at the back
next to a noisy twat
St. George's flag twat
Liveable shit
Liveable shit

Liveable shit – you put up with it
Liveable shit – you put up with it
                        you put up with it
                        you put up with it
                        you put up with it
                        you put up with it

So now I don't dream of anything
I just wait for it to turn up
it's the atmosphere around here
chopped me legs off, look
made me lazy
make me worry about the streets behind me
trees like triffids

no time
the grass is always greener
on the other side
break on through
and end up in a posh cemetery in Paris
"It's not bad."
—*Ya fuckin'…*
Liveable shit

Liveable shit – you put up with it
Liveable shit – you put up with it
                       you put up with it
                       you put up with it
                       you put up with it
                       you put up with it

UNDER THE PLASTIC AND NCT

Ryvita
Ryvita
Crack black pepper

Comrades pick up your arms
the long arm of the lawn is indeed in charge
I won't talk to nice people if they look rich
I know it's not on mate, I'm such a fuckin bitch
surfing comments
lookin' at the likes
whilst the coppers chase bandits through the
    Top Valley skies
to disagree on social networking sites
is to kill the counter-culture
the overturn has died
we pander to the camera
and we want to be observed
we don't get what we ask for
we get what we deserve
stale fags hang on my clothes like indie band badges
as I remember last night ignoring people I don't like
trying to buy a pint
and what does it matter
what if I rot inside a care home
with eight of the bastards

immobile with crap banter
oh look there's Angry J – *wah heeeey!*
Give us a tinkle on the rattling joanna, mate

Under the plastic and NCT
Of grained handmarks devour me
Under the general weight of it all
Exist impossible visions of you

It's one of them innit
the violent exit
let's fuckin' bin it
Ryvita existence
a pointless opposition to the fat
of pointless State resistance
and the State is no longer your voice
the mechanics hijacked by the lies
in false choice of a false fuckin' choice
tied up in death
I hate the terror
the horrible fear
whilst life knifes you as it screams
"You got fuck all left."

Under the plastic and NCT
Of grained handmarks devour me
Under the general weight of it all
Exist impossible visions of you

People might be in groups willingly
let 'em get on with it
you can't expect people to listen to your fucking
mouth just because you don't believe in it
thousands of Saturday lager bellies punching the air
denouncing the value of somebody else's flag
whilst viciously believing in theirs
fucking useless this well-trodden street
vague notions about the so-called elite
and that moulds spit Trent Bridge chaos
it's not really is it?
cardboard heavies
drones to the delusions of a never-never land
where the cross rings out the orders
don't let the mechanics of beer
trick you into thinking you are some kind of warrior
eating barbwire on the wave of violent disorder

Three words:
Cage   Wheel   Hamster

'ere, here's a bit of cheese
– nibble the bastard

Under the plastic and NCT
Of grained handmarks devour me
Under the general weight of it all
Exist impossible visions of love

TISWAS

Pop round Matt, I'll give you a fiver

The land that time forgot, is on repeat
I can hear the screams of people, who wanna be me
They wanna shape my tongue
and tell the others that they were the ones
who made me
who made me
I got called an anarchist
that's for the middle class trainspottists
I don't want my dog on a string
that's gonna hurt the thing
We got jobs and a mortgage plan
an a car with a smoky window down
Blahh! to your life and lob it right up
it don't make sense
I know, look

The dinosaurs are stuck on Denmark Street
the boots of Hendrix lick my feet
I'm not bothered, I never was
here's a crap caravan on Tiswas
The dinosaurs are stuck
no way to get down
the meteor sinks its teeth in the ground

I'm not bothered, I never was
here's a crap gag from Spit the Dog

Cameron's hair dresser got an MBE
I said to my wife, "You'd better shoot me."
It's all gone, what do I do?
Tell my daughter it's not true?
Tell my daughter it's all gone wrong?
Pete Tong, Pete Tong, Pete Tong
Get out the mood dark rays
get out the way
Get out the mood dark rays
get out the way

The dinosaurs are stuck on Denmark Street
the boots of Hendrix lick my feet
I'm not bothered, I never was
here's a crap caravan on Tiswas
The dinosaurs are stuck
no way to get down
the meteor sinks its teeth in the ground
I'm not bothered, I never was
here's a crap gag from Spit the Dog

Tiswas   O.T.T.
Tiswas   O.T.T.
Tiswas   O.T.T.
Tiswas

KEEP OUT OF IT

Charcoal coloured night at the entrance
hazed, I won't walk in
those nights those weekends
give you a kickin'
people half your age
I feel like Elaine Paige
but without the fuckin' tunes an' Joe Cocker bollocks
East miserable Mainline
where the air con won't be saved by Nicolas Cage
put some fuckin' heatin' on
don't be shy
smoker's cough and a poky loo
gets drenched when I turn the tap on
one pint can on

I keep out of it
I keep out of it
I keep out of it
I keep out of it

Play it smooth
too much to consider
—I didn't ask you to, did I?
2 wi one 'o' or two spelt 't' double 'o'
oh no, Speak & Spell hell

Ian's a twat and he still works in a clothes shop
desperately announced any death of whatever
strengthens
better pay ya respects
quick for the kudos
coffees at expensive tea shops
full of local art
—*Fuck off!*
Gromit
Thomas the Tank Engine
Forties sleepy village carrot cake hell
Vomit
his unimagined work towards the goal
of no soul
just happenings
within the four walls of your own fuckin' home

I keep out of it
I keep out of it
I keep out of it
I keep out of it

Eatin' Coffeemate by the spoon
it tastes like cake mix
I waste time flickin' bogeys
really sore nose
"Is this your handywork?"
as the green particles from the men's toilet
land on your fuckin' shirt

I keep out of it
I keep out of it
I keep out of it
I keep out of it

Keep your eyes slit make it
keep your eyes slit, aye
Keep your eyes down to it
Keep your eyes, aye aye

SMITHY

PX CD
SS looks like SS without the line leather
wallpaper in the lift
I still buy your shit
through the eye of a needle
the red blood of history
at your disposal
high heels, Evel Knievel
a picture of Keef lookin' like a twat
who cares about rock stars anymore?
Big leather chairs and panelled walls in Tudor flats
it gave birth to a million street alcoholics
        that you ignore
Ooh, I need a D-string from the guitar store
I'm turnin' over a new leaf
there's no drugs left on this one
plastic belly, "Oooh, my gawd, Sharif."
Opinionated trainees
you've had ya 15 minutes on Facebook
where the garden of splendour fell all over ya
   – you loved it
print the A4 page
print the A4 page …
—*Ah fuck off!*

Sir Paul, you can find binspiration in everything
the recyclable black bins
bags of dog shit
angels sing

New brogues, do a selfie
quick, do it in the design office
this place looks sick
better than your own house
anything's better than ya own house
The Lamp in Sneino is better than your own house
Get a quick giggle out of the unfortunate drinking holes of the lower classes
it's muggins after ten by the angry underclasses
"What y'got?"
"Nothin'."
"Don't look like it."
"Oi, what you got?"
"Nothin'."
"It don't look like it."
Stuck on repeat with a broken nose and robbery
Beat Street

Sir Paul, you can find binspiration in everything
the recyclable black bins
bags of dog shit
angels sing

MIDDLE MEN

New Labour

The metropolis of discontent and lost dreams
Benson and messes and denim jeans
I'm gutted
I didn't think y'would
fly-tippin' down at The Sherwood
the clink of strong drink
racing green paint
crack
Victorian sinks
and flushed is the system
I can't swim so I sink
the earth moves the kerb
it makes the fag areas stink
warp like a tree and bitter twist nicotine we be

Middle men
the metropolis of discontent
red and orange lights and old men
Middle men
the metropolis of discontent
red and orange lights and old men

Monday dinner
Archway
dead the drink of a victim
bad brains
the dead man's milk
Wilko's will have it
they got everything
the dome on the stately home
we got painted in the fumes
from commuters
make my bacon
threaten strangers
with shooters
car stereo shops
that launder dirty dosh
that don't look you in the eye when you walk y'dog
I bet they're all battered in the back on that
hedgehog
sonic
level in ten minutes, two minutes flat
whole bloody fuckin' shop's on it, woah

Middle men
the metropolis of discontent
red and orange lights and old men
Middle men
the metropolis of discontent
red and orange lights and old men

Nine hundred pound for a picture of Debbie Harry
    in art shops
made me laugh my head off
instead with a feelin' of nothin'
floating your ears miss each other
they don't do much
talking like props in a film about *Top Gun*
tears
Top Gun glasses
the new opium for the lasses
rescue dog
like the fuck
the wood catches fire
Patrick Cox loafers
size 10, in brown
loved 'em
out the shop window is still
controlled by the man, lol

Middle men
The metropolis of discontent
red and orange lights and old men
Middle men
The metropolis of discontent
red and orange lights and old men
New Labour

LOAN SHARK

Loan shark
he's gunna take it all
Loan shark
knocking on my door
Jaws of death
he's got a bitter nose
he's gunna take everything I've ever fucking owned

Loan shark
Loan shark
Loan shark

All the peeps
sonic boom
I put the bin out
fruit of the loom
rock'n'roll
nothing's crazy
not a lot is gunna tempt me
no hard-on, no lead
semen
shoot ya fucking face dead
point blank fucker
point blank fucker
fruit of the loom
hard-on pills left in tanks

Hard-on pills left in tanks
and blokes built like brick shithouses
houses'n'houses all blown up
do you mind opening ya door while
I kick the fuck out of ya, look
whats that on ya nose?
I pull the blinds down mate
tread on ya nightmare
twinkle toes
we get the sound down battered
I got a dead head
it's like nothing ever really mattered
I killed a fly with a can of bleach
we get the sound down and battered

Loan shark
he's gunna take it all
Loan shark
knocking on my door
Jaws of death
he's got a bitter nose
he's gunna take everything I ever fucking owned

Loan shark
Loan shark

SLUG TUB

Slug tub
get on the slug tub

Steamy windows on the slug tub
as it slobbers over red lights in crowds
of crap cars and murkish underlight
BA honours, three years
and you've earned the right
to bark at someone, nice
the spice of life
constantly fucking amazes meh
beep, yawn, the new roundabout near work
is responsible for your divorce
I smoke horse
slap a tenner on the brown runner
join the army as a gunner
get ya tits blown off
I used to be a sniper
robbin' handbags down at the Dead Dog'n'Viper
big bloomer
make way for the 10p loaf
that melts when ya try to make toast
a bit more wage is a bit more poverty, obviously
data collection
38 hours a week

I work in the park
empty crisp packets use the runway out on the street
fly my babies, fly
end up on a bench
suntan brown
Monster Munch
ready salted
factor 10 dry

Cry baby cry, every night
he jumps out of his pram for his Angel Delight
Cry baby cry, have you done a poo?
we ain't just 'ere as a nappy for you

Crybaby
I don't mean the pedal
waste lolly on that
be prepared to sink in sandpits
Hello Thor
that twat Dan
he's a moody neighbour
and next door crybabies don't work
you silly doll pram Quaver
rent card
take the key
I been stood in the shop
and the bloke's like
"Where's ya fucking lecky?

It's not gunna charge up on its own –
lay off the weed bad boy
ya flat ain't gunna vamp-up on its own."
Four walls
take a casual stroll down Alfreton Road
past the pawn shop that always looks great
bang up the nitrate like Suede
don't even get near suburban wannabes
squeak when it comes to real gear

Cry baby cry, every night
he jumps out of his pram for his Angel Delight
Cry baby cry baby, have you done a poo?
we ain't just 'ere as a nappy for you

Cry baby cry, every night
he jumps out of his pram for his Angel Delight
Cry baby cry baby, have you done a poo?
we ain't just 'ere as a nappy for you
We ain't just 'ere as a nappy for you, or you
We ain't just 'ere as a nappy for you, or you

We ain't just 'ere
We ain't just 'ere
We ain't just 'ere
We ain't just 'ere
We ain't just 'ere
We ain't just 'ere as a nappy for you

THE COMMITTEE

Drown
Drown

Sad bastards at the Roy Ayers show
one day fans in trendy clothes
jiggin' away to tunes they don't know
big man on steroids
and reputations that don't match up to what
they did in the past
ya tits ain't that stiff Gary – *shut ya mouth*
racist gangsters turn into apologetic weak chancers
we used to run for the club in town
now I play bass in Gil Scott-Heron's band
and past stolen authority
on all that is soul and funk
eager Caesars
get back in ya holes you naughty geezers
nationalisation slaps on the back
ya old fighting chums are thick lads
don't nod at me
like I'm approved Ray Winstone wee wee
stories about machetes in small East End pubs
like bunnies on lettuce
Jackanory that you gimp
he's earned his stripes, mate

look at the limp
brown Saturdays, rainy 1990s
rainy 1990s

Look at the Top Trumps
Look at the Top Trumps
I'm scared – 'ere comes the committee
I'm scared – 'ere comes the committee

The hand fits the glove and you've all lined-up
you were sod all then and ya still nothing duck
you still act like a man
with ya PhD in suedehead stuff and early reggae man
but the boat don't tip
and there's never new ground
you just want people to think
you're a subculture man
hands like goal nets saving everyone
when it's ya 50th birthday, you have a party
in a pub and invite everyone
and walk around like you just wrote 'Jimmy Mack'
—*Fuck off twat*

Look at the Top Trumps
Look at the Top Trumps
I'm scared – 'ere comes the committee
I'm scared – 'ere comes the committee

What needs the machinist
don't even hide the lie
it's a crap machine
no grease, industrial
I got all the cardiacs thinking they are black belts
with a pair of nunchuckers on a box of cereal
Garry Bushell whoopee cushions
under the arse of the next big thing
in breaking glass
you are held down by the hand of the Crown
and the underclass, times two

Look at the Top Trumps
Look at the Top Trumps
I'm scared – 'ere comes the committee
I'm scared – 'ere comes the committee

BRING OUT THE CANNONS

So much
So much

Meanwhile down and way outside
ya dodgy one-liners don't hide what's inside
ya back-up men with planks of wood
who growl at the faces on the racecourse
well if I die, a pipe in my mouth
the banal mess me up
I got mugged by journey south
I got done by Sico's tits
I tried to run, he grabbed me with his mitts
I turned back round and kicked him in the head
X Factor that, dead men said

Bring out the cannons
I bet that fucker called his bluff
we take back what was taken, from us

So much
So much

This ain't any kind of age for the skin of soul
the drains carry rain from the tears of the bold
well in that mate, I took myself off

the grain of the pain in a matchbox
illicit down seams
music box
the depth of the cut makes my record player bop
I plug the thing in
I plug it down tight
the lead gets coiled, coiled right
and tease the cake,
make the cream shake
make the sponge splat all over ya plate!

Bring out the cannons
I bet that fucker called his bluff
We take back what was taken, from us

So much
So much

THE FEAR OF ANARCHY

The concrete as dry as it seems
it ain't no different to the freedom you dream
don't gimme this like ya nitty tat-tat
the street light at night confirmation is that

What does it take to make it all go wrong
why don't you breathe and let the bouncing bomb
  get you
the fear of anarchy
  get you
it runs away from me
  get you
the fear of anarchy
  get you
it runs away from me

I am nothing, no really, really
I am the sunbed under the arse of Philip Green
meat sweats and carpets that fly
the Prince of Persia's got a nice life

What does it take to make it all go wrong
why don't you breathe and let the bouncing bomb
  get you
the fear of anarchy

get you
it runs away from me
get you
the fear of anarchy
get you
it runs away from me

The bouncing bomb
the bouncing bomb
the bouncing bomb
the bouncing bomb

The bouncing bomb of Sodom

Sodom!!!!

The fear of anarchy
it runs away from me

THE MAIL DON'T FAIL

This country's dying scream
squabbling bones
an elite who overlooked the abuse in children's homes
the abuse of human rights for the lust
    of yacht's insides
I can't even spell the word yacht, alright
and if it gets far too much they'll bury the stories with
more abuse on a national scale
The Mail don't fail
it'll gather you like willing subjects
to sow the upset
and turn me into a raving halfwit
on government time
I've got a Westminster mind

A national hero, called Mr Zero
The Mail don't fail
The Mail don't fail

Deidre sez, "You're fat and you're dead."
Body mistakes on frosted flakes
green line on night shift
green lawn on night shift
exhausted voices paying out rates
desk slug, no lettuce

no mates
no chance of an holiday on a rota full of *rigor mortis*
that ain't Latin, that's like it or f'ing lump it
flowers strapped to lamp posts
and bike sprayed white to signify the new ghost
the car that sped angel's delight

A national hero, called Mr Zero
The Mail don't fail
The Mail don't fail

Looks of hate and looks of it's too late
looks of depression and management inefficiency
the guidelines blurred in situations
no clear route matches the expectations
they've all gone
nobody gives a toss
it's all held together by a thin grasp
reason, company ethos, that's where
everybody's snapped in the workhouse lair
"Please Sir, can I have some more?"
I nicked the staff key for the public toilet door
cos the customer one is a real slice of life
dried-up wee on the lid, yeah that's nice
Eamonn Andrews and "This is your life ..."

A national hero, called Mr Zero
The Mail don't fail
The Mail don't fail

Panic attack
panic room
nick nak
paddy wack panic
that's no tie
it's too hot for that
sod it boss
ain't looking three buttons down
I look daps, John Travolta man
one to ones are merely sign it
and get done, nah get down
no Dragon's Den, just dandruff mate
nightmare

SIX HORSEMEN (THE BRIXTONS)

It's the Six Horsemen
And they live in South London
They're so outrageous
They bin doing drugs for ages

The Brixtons, are trying so hard
to be on top of their chaos
The bingo culture – where have you been?
These bastards in the map room, are fuckin'… useless
Players Full House 'ere we go again
No. 10, Maggie's den
The animal farm, employers' blacklist
pivotal, ooh ooh ooh
Johnny Borrell fucks off to an island for four months
at the height of his fame …
was the country bothered?
    – was it fuck
He made a massively bad calculation
    – the thick cunt

It's the Six Horsemen
And they live in South London
They're so outrageous
They bin doing drugs for ages

He likes hardcore
I couldn't give a shit
look at me, all sweating an' shit
pot tit
muffin top
regimental lobbyist punks on slop
twat cap
smashed it in a twat lap
you look at me I look at you
the big other is what makes me and you
we see the same things in sight
and sleep, there is no keep, no line
we are the hands of the shit unspoken
hands of the shit unspoken
we are hands of the shit
shit

It's the Six Horsemen
And they live in South London
They're so outrageous
They bin doing drugs for ages

BUNCH OF CUNTS

Bunch of cunts
bunch of
bunch of fucking absolute cunts
bang banging on the sharpened front
nonplus
the flicker, the fruit machine, the guaranteed bus
and two-for-one
we aren't the sitcom
Ricky, you played it out to the finest crumb on the
armchair, scary!
fresh leaves, morning petrol and sweetie
house, Hansel and Gretel
itch to an hair of *what the fuck*
lost souls in the Victoria Centre look lost bruv
Dr Dre, them headphones are shit
and they're fucking everywhere mate
boom box
urban toss
the ghost of the beaming light
through the fucking beatbox

Bunch of cunts
Bunch of cunts
Bunch of cunts
Bunch of cunts

Hide behind the speaker
bob to the next tune BOOM!
in the jungle the mighty jungle
the lion's off his nut
gold rings, bracelets, years on the road
the SSP went
so I better get the benefit form on the go
I got four, take one *quick*
– I know there's more
we get split
on the endless bar lights, sea side resort
a lump in ya mouth
and bang go the rides the fair ground rides
the screaming crowd
I sound like I got sand paper mouth
touch me thick I'm an Angel Delight
Angel Delight, Farley's Rusks
I want the Spangles right

Bunch of cunts	
Bunch of cunts	just like that
Bunch of cunts	just like that
Bunch of cunts	just like that
	just like that
	just like that
	just like that
	just like that
	just like that

THE DEMON

The Demon
Case it, case it
The Demon
Fanr

Tash and Kalash war men shout their gob off
big smoke fatigues, arsed
You fuckers raise the town to the ground
it's all bollocks – what army?
Smarmy
forget it, you are actually believe it or not,
    the fucking cause of it
Directed – not directed
effected affected
we are thrown around like victims to an
    invading monster from the sea
big claws and it don't knock on doors politely
four coppers hassle one homeless man
    under a poster of Keira Knightley
clear skies, clear lies, and obvious acts of robbery
I used to dabble as a petty thief, but the elite
    do the fucking job properly

The Demon
Case it, case it

The Demon
Fanr

The demon of the wastelands
Shaking staff shoot his enemies down
anyone's up for grabs
death pie tonight for the lads
you volunteer to be the enemies' fear
to be the bomb in the head of a
    fucking kid in bed men
The roots of the woods, small armies bang every day
every paper abuse and fucking murder man
    blahhhhhhhhhhhhh

The Demon
Case it, case it
The Demon

The gratification
the sugar online
I got some twat givin' it the tit grape
giving it the game, bollocks
hard man
ex-solider
that's your fucking problem mate, not mine
shooting what?
ya shooting fuck all
you're just paying for the furniture polish

in the captain's trophy hall
pigs' heads, deers on legs, badgers with a grin
they're all stuffed in the din bin
din tin, tin fuck off min
Auntie Min who hated the relatives in the bungalows
Uncle Charlie picks his fat toes, hobnail boot
I spend my break on the shit shoot
big flavour, smells like tenth spirit
couple of spliffs round the back of Hop Sing
I like a Chinese when I been out drinking

The Demon
Case it, case it
The Demon